The Reagan Range

The Reagan Range:

The Nostalgic Myth in American Politics

James Combs

Bowling Green State University Popular Press
Bowling Green, OH 43403

Books by James Combs

Polpop: Politics and Popular Culture in America

Polpop 2: Politics and Popular Culture in America Today

Published by Bowling Green State University Popular Press

In Loving Memory of

Linus D. Combs

Contents

Preface

"I have always believed," Alexis de Tocqueville wrote to John Stuart Mill, "that the public has the right to ask authors to go to the limit of their powers, and that's a requirement to which, for my part, I try to submit myself." The present author's powers are not in the same league as Tocqueville's, but that esteemed writer is quite right in his admonition. This book, like any other serious attempt at political interpretation of American democratic culture, is ultimately indebted to Tocqueville not only for the profundity of his analysis but also for the inspiration of his example. He approached the new and strange United States with an intensity and interest that was to help shape the seminal and trenchant quality of his work. He proceeded in his study in the spirit of what he called "good sense applied to style." I shall try to proceed in the same spirit, studying the same political culture at a much later date in its history, but with the same intensity, interest and hopefully good sense applied to style.

Tocqueville visited America and began writing his great *Democracy in America* while Andrew Jackson was President. It was, then, during the "Jacksonian Revolution" that his impressions and conceptions of the meaning and fate of American democracy were formed. This book was conceived during and after the election of Ronald Reagan in 1980. Just as Jackson was to become the "symbol for an age," it may well be that Reagan will be an equally symbolic figure (although perhaps not of Jackson's political stature or historical reputation) and also representative of different trends and themes in the American experience. In any case, the present work centers on the idea of Reagan as a representative figure who is amenable to interpretation as something important in the contemporary tides of American political history. Tocqueville's example enjoins us to look at representative political figures in the context of cultural values. If this book can shed any more light on the democratic culture and politics of the United States and

i

the people that political culture chooses to lead, then it will have done so in the Tocquevillean tradition. Even at this late date, we proceed, still indebted to the tradition of one who "performed the task with the air of a half-awakened man marching in the insufficient light of the first dawn." America is no longer at the first dawn of Tocqueville's day, and perhaps its understanding of itself is greater than in the 1830s; but its political knowledge of itself is still imperfect, and the consequences of its political actions are much greater. Hopefully, if the author and reader are awake enough, our joint effort will help insure that we are not as yet at the last dusk.

Introduction
A Theory of Popular Representation

On February 6, 1984, Ronald Wilson Reagan returned to Dixon, Illinois. He had lived in Dixon for several years in the mid-1920s, and his "boyhood home" still stood. Dixon was in competition with nearby Tampico, where Reagan was actually born, for tourist trade, and local promotion by the two towns had a kind of friendly intensity. In Dixon, the Reagan house was restored and "dedicated" for such tourist trade, and a thriving local cottage industry had sprung up, selling postcards, buttons, bumper stickers and other memorabilia. The local industry was given impetus and legitimacy on that bright and cold February day when Reagan toured the house and the town. How much true nostalgic affection he had for the town was impossible to know, since the tour was timed and staged as a media event of his campaign for re-election as President of the United States. He had just announced his candidacy the previous Sunday in a five-minute speech at 10:55 EST carried by the television networks, stressing the theme that "America is back" and that "We have made a new beginning."

The Dixon trip was duly reported by the national news media too. We saw Reagan touring the restored house, reminiscing with local politicos and waving to the assembled crowd. The house was American Gothic, the town vintage Sinclair Lewis Midwest and the people representative of the indigenous American bourgeois ideal. Ronald Reagan had come full circle in his long life, from boyhood in small Midwestern towns through two careers and now back for a staged visit. It was a moment to savor, both for him and for those who study American political culture. At that moment, Ronald Reagan was perhaps at the peak of his personal and political power. His power to command our attention was awesome. At seventy-three, he looked fit and cheerful. His wife was still adoring and loyal. Television and print media with the ability to communicate words and images to hundreds of millions of people

1

around the world recorded virtually his every public word and action and followed him wherever he went. The Dixon trip was clearly manipulated for campaign purposes, but the media were part of the presidential drama; they had to report what he did, because they thought that people wanted to see it. At that moment, Reagan stood at the center of American political consciousness. His popularity was high, the economy was improving, he had stymied and frustrated many of his political opponents, and his re-election seemed certain.

The Dixon trip was a happy occasion, despite its manipulative connotations, and Reagan seemed to genuinely enjoy it. After all, it was a nostalgic trip into his imaginary past, which he called in his autobiography "one of those rare Huck Finn-Tom Sawyer idylls." Dixon was a perfect setting to make that imagined past believable to the millions who saw the image. The simple but comfortable clapboard white house conjured up our collective imagery of the past, of quiet summer nights with safe streets, no pollution and families together in the parlor playing the piano and singing. It was a picture drawn from our popular culture, the River City of *The Music Man*, but also the Zenith of *Main Street* and yes, *King's Row*. If the quintessential small town did not always live up to popular ideals, at least the promise of American life was there, and the people of Dixon apparently believed and celebrated that by their dedication and display of the Reagan house. It was not only an historical monument restored for a quick buck, but also for something more deeply symbolic: the house, and the visit by its now famous and powerful former occupant, represented for them—and perhaps for many of those that would tour the house—something important and extant about their country. The house, as well as the now old man who lived in it long, long ago, was proof of historical and mythological continuity. The man, the house and the occasion became a way of celebrating the popular belief that the past is linked to the present and the present to the future. Reagan's political platitudes seemed quite appropriate in this setting: we are a people who recurrently believe in new beginnings.

Americans invest a great deal of their self-image in the symbolic figure of the President, and Reagan seemed to capture broad currents of popular thought. So much so that many people were capable of forgiving him virtually anything. It astonished many outside of the shared relationship that the majestic office of President, the heritage of Washington and Jefferson and the Roosevelts, was now held by a retired movie actor and television host. Those who doubted his ability and grip on reality were vastly outnumbered by the many who saw in Reagan something attractive and even wonderful. Reagan represented something so fundamentally important that his faults and foibles endeared him to many people all the more. For those who believed in him, blame and error lay elsewhere. Reagan was so right he couldn't possibly be wrong. He embodied a link between past, present and future. For them, he was the symbolic figure of a political age, the leader who gave them hope that we could indeed begin the world all over again, combining youth and maturity, vitality and ancient wisdom, the innocence of the child and the wiser reflection of the sage. He was a national treasure, so valuable that we were willing to spend many millions of our tax dollars on his safety, travels, utterances and health. For those years, we kept him in the permeable cocoon of our political minds, where we could see and hear him.

Reagan's roots in the traditional aspects of national popular life combined with his experience with the latter-day mediated and technological aspects of the way we live makes for an awesome combination. Simply that day in Dixon is a case in point. The day was planned by sophisticated teams of campaign technocrats, experts on the engineering of consent drawn from the various institutions of mass persuasion. The Reagans' itinerary was planned to the last detail by such experts. Highlights of the day were communicated around the world by the most advanced means of communication and taped by the Republican National Committee for future use as campaign propaganda. The Reagans were flown in planes and helicopters and escorted in armored cars that offered the most sophisticated communication and protection equipment. When they left the small town charm of the Midwest, they flew that night to Las Vegas, to be housed in a hermetic hotel penthouse in a sin and glitter capital far from that clapboard house in Dixon.

Las Vegas is a long way in more ways than one from Dixon, but at that time Ronald Reagan seemed to be the only public figure who somehow bridged the many gaps in our national life. His ability to do that had brought him on that day to the apex of his power. His personal command beyond the friendly and intimate confines of little Dixon was awesome. He headed an institutional complex that included the power to start World War III and cause the destruction of many millions of human beings, including most of his own fellow citizens. Decisions made by his Administration affected the lives of not only Americans, but people in places as far-flung as El Salvador and Iran. Soviet-American relations had taken on a new intensity because of him, and over a trillion dollars was being spent on exquisite new armaments, reaching into outer space. His political party planned to spend many millions of dollars for his re-election bid. This included the use of a sophisticated computer directly involved in daily strategic planning of the campaign. Reagan's words and actions were communicated around the world via the Voice of America, and journalists and politicians world-wide heeded and attempted to interpret his every public action. He headed the most powerful country on earth in a period of ongoing world crisis, and his place in world history was secure. His impact on the future of American and world politics was insured, for good or ill, and the legacy of "Reaganism" would earn him either the love or the hatred of many of his countrymen. When one reflected on the political power his country had invested in one man and the global reach that power entailed, it was great indeed.

But for all the trappings of contemporary Presidential power and perquisites, the day in Dixon gave us a glimpse of Reagan's identification with traditionally held themes in American popular culture. His remarks there, like many others of the thousands of speeches he had given to Rotary Clubs, party groups, religious gatherings and so on, were simple articulations of the American creed. He said our national "paralyzing self-doubt" was over and that again, "It's so easy to have faith in America." "Believe me," he predicted, "there are great days ahead for you, for America and for the cause of human freedom." Our strength is "not bullets or balance sheets, but the mighty spirit of a free people under God. And our spirit has never waned. The heart of America is strong, it's good, and it's true. We look forward to the future. We know we were never meant to be second best, and we never will be." He extolled the values and compassion of Americans and recalled the Depression: "Our faith was our strength. Our teachers pointed to the future. People held on to their hopes and dreams. Neighbors helped neighbors...[W]e knew that we would overcome adversity and that after the storm, the stars would come." Dixon has changed, he said, but it hasn't changed in "the values and traditions that made America great." These values "bring us together as a nation. They help us go just as far as our God-given talents will take us. Americans are the most charitable people in the world. We reach out to the need..." The "character" of America can be seen in "small business," the "store down the street," the "faithful who support their churches," indeed "all the brave men and women with faith to invest in the future to build a better America." He extolled "everyday people with big ideas," people with "ingenuity, audacity, and vision," condemned "those who would stifle personal initiative through more and more government" and vowed to "limit the size and scope of the Federal Government" to give "today's pioneers" a chance. He spoke of how our current "rebirth" started "right here, in our homes, schools, churches, and neighborhoods," and that "America has recaptured her drive, energy, and determination." The "new spirit of community" was exemplified in stories of heroism and fundraising for sick children. So, Reagan concluded, he "came home" not to celebrate his birthday, but "to celebrate Dixon and America." He ended with his familiar invocation of "God bless America."

Ronald Reagan was not a man beset by paralyzing self-doubt, and if he was a "great communicator" it was in his ability to imbue such words with the aura of sincerity. Yet his ability to say familiar phrases sincerely would have fallen flat if there were not people out there who wanted to believe them. The "something" that gives continuity and impetus to a political culture was restated by Reagan, both his words and in his being.

There has been surprisingly little attention paid to Reagan's roots in the popular culture of the United States and the relationship of that popular culture to the political culture that Reagan came to dominate in the 1980s. For it is not enough to delineate Reagan's issue and ideological coalition in strictly political terms. Rather more we must understand the broader political context of mythological themes in American culture that Reagan embodies. Reagan was often characterized as a master practitioner of "symbolic politics," but equally often without reference to the mass roots and content of those symbols. A politician cannot play symbolic politics unless there is an audience that wants to see the symbols celebrated. Further, political symbols are culturally specific. They are the language of symbolic action for the political culture of the United

States, and in that sense are part of the story of America as defined by political actors believed in by the mass public. The successful exercise of symbolic politics is not merely an act for its own sake: Reagan's successful symbolic politics had very real consequences both at home and abroad.

It was Tocqueville who first began to understand the intimate interplay of democratic culture and politics in America.[1] Tocqueville saw America as the first mass society, a new kind of egalitarian culture whose politics was to have a logic to it, what we may call the "political logic of democratic culture." This new, egalitarian, anti-aristocratic society would have a new kind of politics, one that would be rooted and constantly have to cater to, the popular myths and tides of opinion held by the masses. America was creating a truly popular culture, and within that cultural context politics would increasingly become a part of that popular culture. The culture of the populace included mass thoughts and actions about politics and made popular culture and political culture inextricably intertwined in a cultural loom that culminates in certain political processes, including the election of popular figures.

Political culturo-logic patterns the ethos, or "character," of a system and disposes it toward certain identifiable trends of recurrent patterns that are consistent with the internal logic of the system. A democratic culture, then, will imbue its political system with certain characteristics consistent with its own culturologic. Public opinion, for example, will play a very large role in such a system, whereas in an autocratic or aristocratic system it would not. The elusive but very real political phenomenon of popular support becomes central to both election and governing. Popular support is garnered by understanding and mobilizing public opinion, including the cultivation of political symbols important to the mass public. Political leaders in a democratic society must celebrate, and in many ways embody, the national mythology that lies at the base of mass public opinion.

Political myths are symbolic representations of group life, placing "us" in an historical drama that includes the realization of group identity and group destiny. In America, of course, much of this was "given" by the Revolution and the sacred documents that defined the republican values of the new state. It also includes the widespread belief in the American Dream, the presumed destiny of America to realize—largely through the efforts of free individuals achieving through possessive individualism—moral and material prosperity in the context of benevolent institutions. The New World was a place of Edenic possibilities, in which the American Adam could create a "City on a Hill" as a moral and material beacon from the Redeemer Nation. America had a manifest destiny to create a new national character and new social order, to enact an historical drama that would lead mankind toward new heights in the march of human progress. Such notions constitute some of the core myths of the American creed. They remain salient aspects of our political mythology, as restated by Ronald Reagan. But in each era the American quest is redefined as a renewed search for the peaceable and prosperous kingdom that is the mythic promise of American life, and no amount of demystifying and even failure undermines the popular mythologic of our national adventure.[2]

Observers of American life have long noted that there is a darker underside to our optimistic and energetic national creed. Tocqueville, for instance, saw the unresolvable tension between equality and achievement, the mad pursuit of distinction yet the desire to be like everybody else, in "the theaters of the unending and agonizing competition among individuals for the attainment of the marks of status" (Nisbet 183). Others have noted our penchant for violence, our desire for conformity, the terrible loneliness engendered by individualism, and perhaps most of all, our roots in Puritan consciousness. Our belief in the rewards of work and punishment for sloth, our ambivalence about wealth, our condemnation of vanity and folly, our narrow pragmatism and our attitudes about sex can be traced to the Puritan heritage. More directly political is our Puritan-derived sense of national destiny as "one nation under God," as a nation blessed by God because of our "covenant" with Him at the beginning. Given that mythic legacy, it is easy to see how Americans can exercise political self-righteousness and see their enemies in Manichean terms, as embodiments of ungodly evil who must be feared and condemned. Critics of the American national mythology have often seen it as dangerous, repressive and haunted by self-doubt.[3]

Both the positive and negative aspects of the American national mythology have been dramatized in literature and life through symbolic figures. For a mythology to become real to people, they have to see it acted out by actors in dramas of cultural significance. In popular literature, mythemes can be represented by simplistic cultural caricatures such as Frank Merriwell, Horatio Alger and Daddy Warbucks, or by more complex indigenous characters such as young Goodman Brown, Captain Ahab, Huckleberry Finn and the great Gatsby. Such latter figures represent the contradictions and depths of what it means to be an American, including the darker tensions wrought by our mythic heritage. From that standpoint, for instance, Hawthorne's Brown becomes a culturally representative figure, "...the prototypical American hero haunted by the obsession with guilt and original sin that is a somber but essential part of America's Puritan heritage" (Guerin 188). On the other hand, there is the more positive image of the "American Adam," a new personality separated from the smudges of the European past to become "...the hero of the new adventure: an individual emancipated from history, happily bereft of ancestry, untouched and undefined by the usual inheritances of family and race; an individual standing alone, self-reliant and self-propelling, ready to confront whatever awaited him with the aid of his own unique and inherent resources" (R. W. B. Lewis 5). The most complicated American heroes, such as Huck Finn, epitomize the "conglomerate paradoxes that make up the American character" (Guerin 190). They represent the value conflicts, contradictions and choices inherent in the American creed. We can identify with their agonies and dilemmas of acting because they are a part of our cultural experience.

This identification also holds when we observe the drama of human relations in actual life. Outsiders in particular have noted the peculiarly contradictory nature of American values and habits. We may hold an attitude while acting wholly inconsistent with it. Perhaps unable to fully resolve value contradictions in our own minds, we identify with cultural heroes who appear able to. We admire the successful achiever who is as the same time able to retain an easy egalitarianism with his peers. We admire the woman who combines family and career. We admire the athlete who is also a scholar. Most of all, perhaps, we admire politicians who represent a resolution of at least some of the values inherent in the national mythology, both in their public personage and in their politics. And even they cannot wholly resolve these contradictions, and indeed they come to represent clusters of values in conflict with other values drawn from our mythology. For we are, as Michael Kammen has argued, a "people of paradox": "Perhaps so many American shibboleths seem to generate their very opposites because they are often half-truths rather than the wholesome verities we believe them to be" (Kammen 273). It is precisely these sorts of mythic inconsistencies that make for political conflict over the interpretation of symbols of moral and material worth. The social and political tensions created by the antinomies of "freedom and responsibility," "liberty and equality," "individualism and altruism" and so on, have made the definition of the American Self difficult and insured that the "quest for the ideal Self" would be unending and variously defined. Conflicts between Americans over whose choice and definition of mythically derived values often become politically salient, and thus politicians attempt to symbolically represent who and what is to be honored.

The Romance of Representation

American mythology treats the unfolding of national history as a "story," a pageant whose origin and destiny is providential. Ronald Reagan, like many political rhetoricians before him, even spoke of a kind of geographic determinism, in which the Deity deliberately placed North America where it is to insure a progressive new chapter in the ancient drama of mankind. American history in this popular view is a splendid and mythic romance, and its various heroes representatives of the mythic values we associated with romantic democracy. Heroes are symbolic leaders who capture the American imagination at a given time because they represent tensions about changing values and circumstances that characterize an age (Klapp, *Symbolic Leaders*). Lindbergh, for example, became a romantic hero of the 1920s because he represented American heroism in a new technological age, dramatizing the values and style of traditional heroism associated with the old frontier into a "new frontier" of technological achievement (the "right stuff" is very old heroic wine indeed) (Ward, "The Meaning").

Political heroes are central to the continuity of romantic democracy by their representation of mythic symbols. Each Presidential hero who captures the political imagination of an age is a "practical demonstration of romantic democracy" (Wecter 486-87). The mix of political and personal characteristics may vary, but the effect is that the Presidential figure becomes in some sense the "symbol for an age." Fisher has summarized this process admirably:

Presidential heroes need to be romantic figures, but they need to be more than that. A romantic figure need only be an adventurous, colorful, daring, and impassioned exponent of certain American ideals, such as individualism, achievement, and success. To be an American hero, one must not only display these qualities, one must also be visionary and mythic, a subject for folklore and legend. The American hero evokes the image of the American Dream, of the ways people and things are when the spirit of America transcends the moment, and her destiny is manifest. The American hero is the symbolic embodiment of this dream in a single person, most predominantly, in certain presidents. (301)

The idea of representation, in both life and art, is a complex but essential concept. A glance at dictionaries and thesari reveals the richness of the term's meanings: artistic likeness or image; dramatic production or performance; one person standing for another, or for a multitude or constituency; personification or impersonation; image, icon, or facsimile. So the concept of representation has the root sense "re-presentation," a making present again, the nuance suggested by the "re-" prefix: "again, anew, retell"; to "re-present" something means to present it again. In this regard, Hannah Pitkin has pointed out that:

representation taken generally, means the making present *in some sense* of something which is nevertheless *not* present literally or in fact. Now, to say that something is simultaneously both present and not present is to utter a paradox, and thus a fundamental dualism is built into the meaning of representation.... But there is no need to make mysteries here; we can simply say that in representation something not literally present is considered as present in a nonliteral sense. (8-9)

It is in this "nonliteral sense" that a Presidential personage becomes the momentary "symbolic embodiment" of the mythic heritage of romantic democracy. Political representation at this level is dynamic, a process that links the specious present with the cultural memory to which it is heir and the anticipated future that is always so problematic. Political reality is always in a present, containing both elements of continuity and discontinuity, and existing as a temporary political process which must be dealt with if continuity is to prevail (Mead; Maines). As with Lindbergh, a representative figure is used in the present to link that time and place with the past and the future. A Presidential hero is similarly an agent of political mediation, becoming the symbolic mediator of political change by successfully linking past, present and future in his politics. A "symbol for an age" mediates the historical process through representation of continuous mythemes from the past through the present and into the future.

In the national political drama that is at the center of American culture, Presidents have the possibility of becoming representative figures whose symbolic significance goes far beyond simply being the chief executive of the national State. For political elites in a democratic culture serve functions that are not strictly speaking political. A political leader in a society in which public opinion is predominant becomes an object of mass identification. In the changing world of a dynamic democratic culture, there is a "collective search for identity" (Klapp, *Collective Search*). The mass search for a socially confirmed concept of self activates them to seek identity cues from symbolic leaders. Given the right combination of cultural and temporal characteristics, such identification can focus on a President as the symbolic embodiment of those mass fantasies about self. The political actor of the national stage becomes the communicator of a social identity with which significant parts of the mass public identify. This identification means that the actor personifies some set of cultural attributes and actions that provide mass audiences with intellectual and emotional satisfaction. Successful group leaders are representative of their followers by being perceived as "one of us" (having membership characteristics of those he/she would lead); as "most of us" (representing the modal or normal beliefs and habits of a group, reflecting moods and emotions at a particular time); and as the "best of us" (but not too much so), an exemplar of us, the surrogate father of us, the hero of us (Kretch 438-39). "Full of pride and without enlightenment," noted Tocqueville with aristocratic disdain, "the voters wish to be represented by people of their own sort."

So in this sense political representation in a democratic culture is part of the broader process of popular representation. For the popular culture of such a society seems to create a wide variety of symbolic leaders ranging from comic to tragic figures. Such figures serve the broader function of popular mediation, dramatizing what's happening so that people can see what it is that they are supposed to figure out. Radio comics during the 1930s Depression, for instance, mediated mass fears and fantasies about that time through humor, reassuring radio audiences that everybody was in the same boat, that things will improve and that the Roosevelt Administration was trying its best (Wertheim). Our quest for social identity leads us to seek out representative figures from popular culture with which we may identify. The modern phenomenon of celebrity, for example, is one of pervasive "artificial social relationships" with which we provide ourselves identity cues (Caughey). The celebrity represents symbolic embodiments of cultural identities and values. This has been insightfully recognized by Richard Schickel in his book on Douglas Fairbanks, Sr. He notes that the popular phenomenon of celebrity emerged in an era in which "the public ceased to insist that there be an obvious correlation between achievement and fame." For the first time, "it was possible to achieve 'celebrity' through attainments in the realm of play." Now Americans had "two realities" to contend with; the "separate reality" of celebrity involved us with personages in a pseudo-environment with whom we were profoundly related and about whom we knew and cared more than most people in our daily "real" lives. Schickel then reaches a startling conclusion:

It is not too much to say that we have, in about half a century's time, reached a point where most issues, whether political, intellectual, or moral in nature, do not have real status—that is, literally, the status of the real—until they have been taken up, dramatized, in the celebrity world...[I]t is now essential that the politician, the man of ideas and the nonperforming artist become performers so that they may become celebrities so that, in turn, they may exert genuine influence on the public....It is their way of moving over from the realm of the ordinary reality to that other reality, that surreality (the word literally means super-reality) which is peopled exclusively by the well-known....It is in this surreal world that all significant national questions are personified and then dramatized...[T]o a greater degree than we allow ourselves to suppose, the quality of celebrity 'acting' while in view of the media is a large—perhaps the largest—factor in determining national goals. (Schickel, "Fairbanks")

In this view, the celebrity is not only a popular representation, but also potentially a representation of other areas of public discourse, such as politics.

Yet the interplay of popular and political representation does in some way antedate the advent of modern popular culture and celebrity. For mass audiences likely do not separate cultural dramas into such neat and exclusive categories. If our thesis is correct about the mass desire to witness representative figures in cultural dramas, then the social process at work is the production of popular art, be they the artifices of popular media or the artifices of political arenas. What Norman O. Brown says about political representation applies to popular representation as well: "Political representation is theatrical representation. A political society comes into existence when it articulates itself and produces a representative; that is to say, organizes itself as a theater, addressed to a stage, on which their representatives can perform" (111). The magical romance of social theater becomes the root social process of representation. The artifice of social theater becomes the objective representation of subjective experience, and subjective experience becomes the source of dramatic representation. Both popular art and political artifice are only possible with "the aesthetic illusion of distance" (Brown 120). So popular and political cultures are built, sustained, and changed with the representations that people create and believe.

The popular determinants of political representation in America actually go back before the invention of the movies and television. It really is rooted in what we may term the "Tocquevillean principle"—the strain toward popularization in which "public opinion, viewed as the transitory general will, is regarded as the *immediate* as well as the ultimate arbiter of all matters of policy and taste" (Kornhauser 28). The Toquevillean principle is central to culturo-logic, in which the standard of popular choice, the extension of the principle of democracy, is increasingly valued and applied. Tocqueville grasped what the implications of such a culture are—the passion for bourgeois equality, the sanctity of individual pursuits, the translation of majority rule into "the tyranny of the majority," the discovery of lowest common denominators, and so on. In such a culture, political life would not be the least of the "democratic arts," by discovering and celebrating representative figures who win offices such as the Presidency as symbolic embodiments of the values and moods of public opinion.

Symbol for an Age

It is a mistake to regard politics as an adjunct to "material" politics, or as something that is less effective in the exercise of power. Presidential figures who achieve the status of a Reagan do not do so simply through the successful creation of economic prosperity and security. Rather more, through their symbolic representation of popular mythology Presidents acquire the temporary status of democratic king. The Presidency, after all, was given original definition by George Washington, who represented in his political personage not only the values of the Revolution but also popular mythemes of rectitude and service. The congeries of images associated with Washington—military hero, Father of his country, the child who could not tell a lie, Cincinnatus as President, apotheosis in classical statuary—gave impetus to the importance of the President as symbolic leader and recurrent popular investment in figures who could embody what a particular political time regarded as valuable (Wills; Scwartz). Not every President nor every political time calls for popular investment in a President as "symbol for an age," but it is a recurrent impulse to give definition to politics by identifying popular will with the current President.

We do not fully understand the process of historical recurrences and cycles, but it does seem clear that political cultures of long duration go through discernible and identifiable periods and that these periods bear resemblance to previous periods is more than coincidence. When we speak of "ages of reform" or a "decade of reaction" we have in mind historical referents that invite comparison. Political cultures develop and cherish mythemes that help define the "story" of the political order, but mythemes may be given different definition and emphasis in alternative political periods. In American political history, we seem to go through recurrent periods of political respite that follow the political exhaustion and disillusionment of a previous political age. Such periods are "reactionary" in the sense that there is a symbolic search for, and celebration of, "fundamentals" that it is thought we have strayed from. These political eras are often characterized as "conservative," attempting to reinvest new meaning into ancient symbols and touting the authority of the mythic past. In that sense, it is fair to call them "nostalgic," in that there is an acute sense of a temporal division between a prelapsarian world of mythic time and a current postlapsarian world that must be reacted against and "renormalized." Those caught up in such movements of symbolic redemption may become disillusioned or simply exploitative, but the political dynamic at the moment of their creation is the restoration of the symbolic ascendancy of hierarchy and habit that is fundamentally sound. But the temporal momentum of such periods seems always to develop into something static and defensive, attempting to "hold the line" against historical process and deny historical failure. For popular politics, the real importance is as a respite in the wake of exhaustion and in the dread of anticipated further change. The impulse is to suspend political conflict, mute criticism and debate, attempt to re-establish a world with coherent internal logic, assert national and moral superiority and imagine the romantic eternity of normalcy.

Recurrent periods of metapolitical respite are presided over by an anachronistic figure who invites mythic association with romantic democracy. In many ways, however, the figures we have in mind—Grant, Harding-Coolidge, Eisenhower and Reagan—are pale reflections of the original Presidential symbol for an age, Andrew Jackson.

In his famous book, *Andrew Jackson: Symbol for an Age*, historian John William Ward interpreted the Presidency of Jackson as a political representation of romantic democracy. Jackson was president during one of the axial periods of democratic change and the creation of popular culture in America. When we speak of the "age of Jackson," we do so because Jackson dominated not only through institutional power but also popular power as a representation of the values and aspirations of his constituents. Jackson was a practical demonstration of the validity of romantic democracy by the popular image then of who he is, by the mix of fact and legend about him in the common imagination that made his supporters identify with him. "Through Andrew Jackson," writes Ward, "the American people were vicariously purged of shame and frustration. At a moment of disillusionment, Andrew Jackson reaffirmed the young nation's self-belief; he restored its sense of national prowess and destiny." But the national celebration of self-love that focused on Jackson augured the process by which the abstraction of "nationalism" was "articulated in terms of Andrew Jackson, so that Andrew Jackson became a counter for the ideas themselves." Jackson gave palpable and immediate substance to national myths-in-the-making, human form to as yet nascent beliefs. But national pride was now focused on the political personage of the age, and Jackson would be the personification of the mythemes of "Nature," "Providence" and "Will." The stories and images that would prevail about Jackson centered around those mythemes, and no amount of debunking and criticism then or now could shape their popular veracity; as Ward notes, "...we are in the area of imaginative play, which is less concerned with history than with objectifying concepts which are the chief supports of culture."

Jackson was an original, a model of popular power that invited admiration and emulation. After the Presidencies of those associated with the revolutionary generation—the Virginia Dynasty and the Son of John Adams—Jackson was a popular innovation, an authentic hero who represented in his political personage emergent mythemes held by the common man, now the sovereign voter. Jackson was a symbol of romantic democracy, personifying the political logic of democratic culture. As a "symbol for an age," he served both dramatic and didactic purposes. He dramatized through his ascendancy the triumph of the "common man" and the liberal capitalism and bourgeois aspirations that gave force to the Jacksonian movement. And he was a model for emulation, symbolic proof positive that the American genuine self could incorporate in his being both equality and achievement, democratic faith and romantic heroism, wisdom and innocence. Jackson was a man of action and accomplishment, but the translation of his personage into a popular symbol was to serve as a precedent for other Presidential aspirants who hoped to capture the popular imagination to that extent. Not every attempt succeeded, but when the political time and the personage cohered, a successor to the Jacksonian phenomenon was found.

But the periods and figures we have in mind differed from the Age of Jackson. The Jacksonian Age was creative. But the Ages of Grant, Harding-Coolidge, Eisenhower and Reagan were re-creative, political interludes following a time of political intensity and exhaustion. Grant was a respite following the Civil War and Reconstruction. He was obviously not a figure of the stature of Jackson, but he was a symbolic figure who represented an important desire for a period that renormalized the world. Grant was expected to preside, to serve as a model for popular power not in the sense of action but rather in the sense of passive restoration of peace and prosperity. He represented the impulse toward a non-political politics following the tumultuous events of the previous decade. The Grant Administration was scandal-ridden but permissive of capitalist expansion and lost some of its aura of complacent normalcy after the Panic of 1873. But Grant's definition of the Presidential role, and the country's acquiescence in an interlude period, gave sufficient shape to an atemporal time. Grant had a genius for political imperturbability and reluctance for involvement; he was "disengaged" from controversy and policy-making. Like

Jackson, he was a military hero who initially conjured up nostalgia for past heroics. But Grant as President was a ludenic hero, a Head of State characterized by inanition. After Lincoln and Andrew Johnson, the inane was the preferable approach to presiding over metapolitics.

The Grant era was a "play period" that succeeded in imposing a static definition of political reality. It tried half-heartedly to undo some of the changes (in the status of blacks, for instance) wrought by war and upheaval, but mainly it ignored conflict and concentrated on supporting business. Grant himself was a lesser romantic figure than Jackson, but dutifully conducted the rituals of power as if the world were normal again. Political normalcy was an act of will, focusing attention on the still eye of the hurricane. Grant made a political romance out of democratic normalcy by making the Presidential task one of ritual play. Ritual play was not only a substitute for real action, it was an agency of political romance. The romantic temper in democratic politics exalts the symbolic, representing the puerility of common life and aspirations as themselves heroic and exalting the dream of normalcy as established and eternal. Grant's failures in administrative and economic matters were outweighed, in his apparent continuing popularity, by his achievement in symbolic politics. His conception of the Presidency as a popular representation who conducts ritual celebrations of symbolic power was to become a recurrent motif of future Republican regimes.

The Harding-Coolidge regime of the 1920s had much in common with Grant. Harding came to power in the wake of war and upheaval with a mandate to restore normalcy to "the American village." Although beset by scandal and eventually depression, Harding-Coolidge was a stable regime supported in its ritual conduct of symbolic play. Harding was a virtual representation of babbittry, the dominant heroic business type of the age; Coolidge was the solemn high priest of unreflective acquisition and leisure. Both utilized nostalgic mythology in order to assure that the past has relevance in the present and that the popular power of romantic democracy was intact. If Harding evoked the bloviating gregariousness of the small town Rotarian, Coolidge seemed the epitome of the taciturn New England schoolmaster. But like Grant, they were passive and tolerant models of power, ritual celebrants of beneficent plutocracy, evoking the magic of the marketplace and the mystery of familial community as the source of popular authority. As chief magistrate, they saw the role of government as primarily symbolic and their own role as one of the celebration of values, not the satisfaction of interests. They presided over a weak government but a strong State, providing a relaxed tolerance of private cupidity and consumption while exhorting the symbolic power of progress.

Coolidge was a stolid anachronism who represented traditions of romantic democracy while the business ascendancy of the 1920s was destroying them. But like Grant, he provided temporal mediation, assuring that the prelapsarian world of preindustrial mythic time was still informing the brave new world of the present. The representation of the myth of democratic normalcy now restored becomes the occasion not only for political passivity but also for economic and moral innovation that is definitely postlapsarian. Coolidge could preach the redemptive doctrines of prelapsarian rectitude with the air of a Puritan minister, but his ritual celebration of the sacred did not invite political intervention to redeem the profane of Wall Street or Main Street. Like Grant, the Harding-Coolidge Era was ahistorical and against the use of political power as an agent of history. It was not an "eternal return," reuniting cosmos and history; rather more it was a rhythmic interlude that denied the temporal and practical gap between the prelapsarian and postlapsarian universes. It was a return only to primitive political communication, the sound fundamentals that themselves became anachronistic when they began to ring hollow and unrealistic after 1929.

Eisenhower was both military hero and prelapsarian anachronism who came to power in the midst of political tension and violent conflict. "Ike" was a perfect representation of romantic democracy and presided over an age of political stability and economic growth. His administration ended in scandal, international tension and recession, but his popularity remained high and his status as symbolic leader secure. Like Grant and Coolidge, Eisenhower was able to preside as an unknowledgeable innocent, authentic and sincere but not thoughtful nor political. As the nation moved further away from its mythic origins, he was able to celebrate the romance of simple gifts while forging the "corporate commonwealth" of the military-industrial complex and the international alliances of empire. Like his predecessors, whatever political skill he had was hidden from view, with his public role largely confined to ritual celebration. As with Grant and Coolidge, Eisenhower evoked a personal image of puerile innocence, while political complexity and guilt swirled around him. But such a role definition is crucial for political normalcy. The 1950s, like the post-Reconstruction period and the 1920s, was anything but placid. But the Presidential role is atemporal, denying as an anachronistic personage the unrelenting reality of time. Eisenhower was a figure who was prelapsarian and therefore timeless, who for the 1950s could not have been more timely.

Given the accidents and vagaries of political history, the periods we have in mind do seem to have much in common. The dominant political figure of the age is someone who acts as an analogic authority, someone who represents the widespread desire for a comfortable and congruent spell that is neither innovative or reflective. His Presidential authority is rooted less in the political power of a coalition of interests than in his familial image as an avuncular symbol of tranquility and security. Grant, Coolidge and Eisenhower were personages celebrated for their place in cultural romance and the genius of their political innocence. The analogy they evoked was that of an archaic authority whose presence and principles in the present defeated time because of their status. They were from another time and place and brought their experience with a mythic or heroic age to a present popular age, which accorded them the presiding power of popularity. Their political being was complete before the present they ruled, so they were not expected to grow, learn, or agonize in an office momentarily defined as ritualistic. But in all three cases, they were easily re-elected and remained popular precisely because of their correct definition and conduct of the Presidential role. In that sense, Grant, Harding-Coolidge and Eisenhower must be counted as Presidential successes. They served a valuable public function: they restated the myths of the State and indeed became the mystic representation of their symbolic power. An analogic authority re-presents the metaphor of the legitimacy of popular order, the myth of eternal normalcy rooted in the democratic power of a stable and just social hierarchy. They head a mythological coalition that turns the emotional quest for certainty into a Presidential image of monumental but familial imperturbability, with a kind of inaccessible accessibility.

These similar political periods, then, are times of Presidential ritual play. The political task of the leader is the re-establishment of the myth of normalcy through mystification. Ritual enactment of the political role serves the purpose of exemplifying and symbolizing the political bonds which comprise the legitimated order. Political rituals are metaphors of power, so proper enactment of both sacred and mundane activities serve as a figurative and tacit comparison between what is ritualized and the larger social order. The ritualist symbolizes the right and good political habits and confirms what those habits should obtain throughout a normal system. Our Presidential ritualists were conventional symbols who framed the political universe as part of common normalcy. They mediated time and circumstance through political play that made them into aesthetic figures above politics. They were masters of political normalcy, communicating messages of truth and right through their archetypical role. They became symbols for an age by immersing their public selves in the liminal dream-state of a symbolic world. They represented things which were above and beyond mere prosaic politics. They did not dominate the literal political world, but rather the poetic world of political play. They were representations of political ludenics—play-heroes in a surreal and supersensible realm of analogical romance. They presided over a political interlude that simulated normalcy through Presidential symbolic play. The simulation of the essential political pattern of "normal" relationships does not correspond with either manifest or latent patterns in the temporal inheritance and emergence of the time, but does produce a period of political quiescence and pause. The desire for such a period invites such a political stance, celebrating the past and assuring the future while ignoring the present. Such Presidential representation, then, is appropriate for a time of interludic normalcy; it would not be appropriate for a period of either catastrophe or movement, which call for instrumental action. But it is enough of a recurrent precedent to suggest the historical "appropriateness" of Ronald Reagan for the 1980s.

Ronald Reagan and Romantic Democracy

We may best understand Ronald Reagan through his critics. He was a political anachronism, they said, someone associated with nostalgia, unable to understand the currents and subtleties of contemporary history. He was dated and simple-minded, they charged, lacking the experience and knowledge required of the Presidential task. He had no heroic qualifications, no ability to deal with political change, no talent for political learning. What his critics did not understand is that these qualities, or lack of them, come to be virtues when the appropriate political moment arrives. An anachronism is seen as having archaic ties that anchor the present. Nostalgia becomes a link to something we fear we may have lost but can recover, or at least celebrate, in a present. Being dated suggests no complicity in the fallen condition of the present, and quite the contrary connotes temporal experience of a prelapsarian condition that might redeem the quagmire of now. Espousing the maximology of simple truths comes to be seen as the height of wisdom, the kind of clarity of thinking the fuzzy present has unfortunately lost.

Reagan's electoral successes and personal popularity rather suggest the confluence of a political age and an analogic authority to preside over it. It was the present that was "dated," however late we may feel it to be in the American story. Reagan was the personage of the 1980s who, however unwittingly, became the popular being who represented the logic of representation. However we may define the rhythms of political time that gave us previous "renormalized" eras, by 1980 Ronald Reagan was a political representation whose time had arrived. Like previous political ages, the stage for the appearance of a figure associated with the heroism of romantic democracy was set by the turbulent movement of the 1960s devolving into the rancor and confusion of the 1970s. Reagan was the benefactor of the inability of a succession of Presidents to command the waves. The newly defined reality of Reagan's political metaphysics was that some waves did not exist and the ones that did exist could safely be ignored or defended against. The logic of atemporal political representation focuses on a Presidential drama of political normalcy, a dream-space at the center of a political reality where the waves do not intrude. Like King Canute, the act of commanding and not the actuality of command was enough. The call is not for real solutions, but for romantic answers.

Like his predecessors, Reagan's political romanticism was a dream-picture of normal life, a stable social hierarchy given microcosmic imagination by the aesthetic conduct of Presidential government. It was not a vision of heroically ascending movement or apocalyptically descending catastrophe. Rather it was a romance of normalcy that excluded the possibility of catastrophe and denied the necessity of movement. Following what now constitutes a tradition, and perhaps a strategy, the Reagan Presidency was a ritual of power. Like Grant, Harding-Coolidge and Eisenhower, the exercise of power was in fact restrained and modest; the passive and positive style stymied ambitious agendas of reactionary revolution or social discipline. Reagan himself was no less a ludenic hero than the others. His authority derived from his association with, and memory of, mythic romance; his analogic status was enhanced by his experience in, and learning from, our primary institution of mythologic celebration; and his success derived in large measure from his ability to reimpose romantic categories on nation and office. His impeccable performance of the rituals of power projected an image of a normalized political center that symbolized the restoration of stable social hierarchy. The Reagan Presidency gave ritual coherence to an interludic time by grounding power in the familiarity of Reagan's presence. The Presidential political existence becomes the central defining motif of such an age, making the President a metaphor for power, or more precisely, a metaphor for the assumptions and conduct of power that are to characterize and permeate society. This may range from the celebration of the acquisition and display of wealth to the reassertion of the symbols of status honor and degradation to the invocation of God's blessing on mythic institutions, but at the static center the President stands as an unencumbered vessel of political disengagement. Reagan was the symbol for a disengaged age that depended upon his ludenic knowledge, fantastic character and ritual performance for sustenance.

Reagan, then, was not a figure without precedent. He was no anomaly nor accident. But obviously he was not identical with comparable predecessors. His ludenic knowledge of popular mythology and maximology was enhanced by his cumulative popular experience, an advantage in popular communication often denied generals. His fantastic character stemmed not only from the usual reconstructed Huck Finn roots and Horatio Alger ascent, but also from being an integral part of our fantastic movie experience. Coolidge was part of the Our Town fantasy—the President as mayor/minister/stage manager—that made him a "Puritan in Babylon,"

but Reagan's fantastic breadth of popular being made him part
of the range of ludenic heroism that Hollywood created. His ability
to conduct the Presidency as a ritual performance was smoothed
by long experience in the ceremonies of celebrity. In these senses,
his Presidential role enactment was superior to and more
sophisticated than those of his historical precedents.

It is true that all Presidents are in some sense symbolic leaders,
put upon a national pedestal and celebrated for their representation
of the democratic faith. But a figure like Reagan seems appropriate
for a certain kind of time, a time wherein political reality is defined
more by perception than event. Reagan ruled over a romantic state,
an heroic state of grace that was a creation of the power of will.
The romantic state is a re-enchanted order, a symbolic reality with
idealized qualities that separate it from the processes of politics
and the ideology of "realism." If the realist wished to use politics
to manipulate fact, the romantic transforms politics into aesthetics.
The realist claims to be instrumental; the romantic exalts the poetic.
The realist points to the prosaic sources of power in a coalition
of interests; the romantic celebrates the power of unified wills in
a mythological coalition. Realistic power derives from the secular
technoeconomic and political orders; romantic power derives from
the sacral and mystic. In an era of political romanticism such as
the 1980s, then, there is concentration on the symbolic, focus on
the conduct of ritual dramas that celebrate and romanticize political
symbols and identification of a symbolic leader who represents the
re-enchantment of the State. In that ironic sense, Ronald Reagan
was the ultimate statist, a political ritualist who sang the glories
of the romantic state, reinvoking its organic unity with the other
but subordinate institutions of the Union, appealing to the sanctity
of the State as the foundational reaffirmation of meta-authority.
Such reinvestment of collective faith gives credence to the cult of
the State, characterized by uncritical acceptance of the idea that
the State can achieve aesthetic perfection through sanctified action.

If it is the case that the Reagan era does resemble past romantic
regimes, then the spell is ultimately always broken with the
reassertion of mundane political process. It may even be the case
that periods of political romanticism contain the seeds of their own
destruction. The political romantic defines reality as a creation that
can be brought into existence by the mystery of ritual celebration.
But it is more likely the case that temporal reality has a logic

independent of human will, Machiavellian *fortuna* that is in the long run beyond symbolic or even instrumental control. Like his predecessors, Reagan's celebration of the symbols of democracy and capitalism were to return, like ghosts conjured at a political seance, to haunt their conjurer.

Ronald Reagan, then, was a political figure of considerable complexity. His biographers and journalistic observers of his life and political career have treated various aspects of his personality and actions, but they have not, I think, adequately touched upon what we have tried to say about him briefly here: what did this man have that made him for a time the political darling of a nation? What forces in our national past and present gave him the power and reputation to become what he became? We have suggested here that he was both precedented and unprecedented, and that the study of what he means, as a popular and political being, tells us much about ourselves. He was a phenomenon (in the Greek root of that term, "that which reveals itself"), but not necessarily a mystery. His appeal, conduct and fate can be demystified through analysis. We here will have to interweave different strands of analysis to achieve the depth of description that enhances our understanding of what he meant as a politico-cultural phenomenon.

To the end of understanding Reagan in this kind of context, I want to discuss the symbolic configuration of nostalgia he seemed to represent. I contend that Reagan's appeal had much less to do with the adventurism of the mythic West than the mythic normalcy of the Town. The locus of American normalcy is situated in "the country of our mind" between the wilderness and the city, in the place that Reagan described in his speech that day in Dixon. It is a place of human scale, of moral and material prosperity, of civic pride and value consensus. The Town's institutions—the Family, the Business and the Church—are the normalized ways of realizing what Reagan liked to call "the good things" of American life. Those good things are the province of the Town, the place of Reagan's mythic origins and the cradle of the values he was so eager to remind us of. To understand the political phenomenon of Ronald Reagan, we must understand these popular roots. Like him, we must return to the Town.

Chapter One
The Town

The United States is not chronologically a very old country, so it created its own mythology as the country grew. Washington was venerated as a demigod in his lifetime; the dime novel created the myth of the Wild West as it was being settled; Horatio Alger heroes emerged in popular literature in the dynamic phase of capitalist industrialization. The quickness and harshness of the settlement of the continent and the subsequent growth of the nation into a gigantic power gave impetus in the popular mind to transforming the process into romance. The logic of popular romantics favors the creation of a methodology of heroic ascent into a state of eternal stability. Living happily ever after is preceded by a period of struggle in a mythic time that concludes in the triumph and establishment of a peaceable kingdom. Romantic dreams stem from anxieties about national motives and moral purpose becoming the stuff of popular mythological history. National history becomes an aesthetic narrative of metaphorical figures and events who enact the pageant of America unfolding as a benevolent force in the world. We create mythic times of strife and triumph (the Revolution, the Civil War, World War II) and alternative periods of idealized domestic peace. Both serve as metaphors and models to emulate or celebrate in the diminished and unfinished present and support the underlying romantic myth of aesthetic perfection.

It is the nature of political time that we are always in a present, a defined "now" with its own definition of the presentational predicament. Politics involves dealing with the temporal unfolding of events. We use referents from either the past or the future as a guide to understanding the present. The future lets us project what is happening into time to come and either act to affect the future or resign ourselves to the futility of action and accept what comes. The latter is a classical view of fatalistic resignation; the former is a realistic belief in action rooted in the myth of progress.

But as we have noted, political convulsions and the accumulation of political time play havoc with the belief in progress and give impetus to using the past as a mythic referent. In both cases, people are likely searching for a metaphor of consolation, relating a representation from a time not now as a model for what is not. For those oriented toward the future, such an image invites action. For those oriented toward the past, the vision invites ritual celebration. Those who act need the consolation that action assures the future, and they need to imagine a "then" that is the result of their activity now. Those who celebrate the past invoke it in a present that has fallen from a state of grace. Even if they offer the past as a metaphor for action, there is no certainty given that we can recover the past in the future. The future-oriented believe in a romance of ascent, while the past-oriented believe in a romance of descent. But descent suggests irrecoverable loss, the uncertainty of recovery and redemption and the likelihood of further drift from the model. Hope that the descent can be halted, the past made the future, the "country turned around," is always dashed by the recalcitrance of time. In that case, the postlapsarian world always fails the prelapsarian. This is a vision of history not as up or down, but as before and after. Since we now live in the after, those who celebrate the before have the consolation of knowledge of mythic time and place. Their vision is retrophetic rather than prophetic, predicting the past rather than the future. Anticipating the past lessens responsibility for, and allows contempt of, the present and by extension prevents nostalgia for the future.

It was commonplace to relate Ronald Reagan to "the politics of nostalgia." It was clear enough that he struck a responsive chord by his self-association with the prelapsarian world that persisted in popular memory after the bitter historical herbs of recent decades. Not only has the United States now acquired a past that included complicity in difficult and inconclusive political experience, but it also possessed a dreadful sense of political and cultural "lateness" and imperial decline of "the American century." As in previous political ages, doubt was cast on the myth of progress as an inevitable product of techno-economic innovation and national power. Such doubts threaten both motivation and stability, auguring a systemic crisis. But by the time of Reagan, the predicaments and disappointments of history seemed also to include a sense of "the disenchantment of the world," the accumulative and widespread conception found both in popular attitudes and art, of the devaluation of values that logically might lead to the delegitimation of institutions. Reagan's task, then, was doubly difficult: not only was he charged with the renormalization of the center of the world, he also had to fight the creeping feeling that the American story was close to being over and that the enchantment the idea of America had once connoted was now irrevocably lost. Reagan, unlike Eisenhower or others, had to re-enchant the world, to imbue the profane present with the aura of the sacral past in order to forestall or reverse the rapid decomposition of value orientations. Reagan had to remind us of the secular theodicy of romantic democracy as the monumentic referent of re-enchantment. His task was the appropriation of popular memory in the service of political stability and economic power. Symbolic enchantment serves the cause of a stable social hierarchy through the reaffirmation of myth and the denial of historical diminishment.

Reagan's project involved the peculiarly American tension between power and innocence. Americans are always losing their innocence while proclaiming that they remain innocent of historical guilt and moral culpability. Yet our vast imperial power and sense of fallenness nags at us. We once occupied a "virgin land" and saw ourselves as a new world. The dream of romantic democracy is of a world of innocent power, or more precisely, power exercised by the innocent, insuring both purity of motive and benacity of result. Imagining ourselves as the sacralized heirs of the enchanted world of romantic democracy not only provides mythic self-justification, it also suggests continued self-possession. The ideal self in a society committed to innovation is always in danger of becoming "Protean" to the point of unrecognizability, so the reassertion of qualities of cultural self in heroic roles serves a renewed sense of a grip on the definition of Self that "made this country great." The power of political or economic action can involve guilt if not imbued with sanctification, so the reassertion of innocence, or powerfulness freed of the taint of evil, offers the consolation of self-righteousness. Righteousness justifies the possession of power and wealth in the fallen postlapsarian world not by reference to ideology or necessity but rather mythic history. The personage who represents the happy union of power and innocence must convey historical consciousness, giving him an aura of self-righteousness acquired in primal experience. It is that experience which inspires the confidence thought needed to sustain systems of power, for whatever else such a stance may sacrifice in humility and proportion.

It is this fundamental problem of sustaining confidence in extant systems, then, that gives credence to the politics of nostalgia. The nostalgic (from the Greek *nostos*, "return home") is a rampart between past and present, an imagined link between the microcosmic and the macrocosmic, the infinite and the finite, the realm of metachronic symmetry and diachronic asymmetry. The nostalgic past is of use to us because it has a structure, a set of idealized institutions that function in a harmony lost somehow by error, folly, or forgetfulness. Our charge by the nostalgic politician is not simply remembrance lest we forget to honor the dead, but to claim that the dead is not moribund and rather has a valid and vital claim on the living. Political nostalgia is not only a mass exercise in wistful trips to bountiful "good old days," wherein the present suffers by contrast with the past. The psychic root of nostalgia may lie in regretful fantasy, but in periods of vulnerability it can be used for the political purpose of directing behavior into approved roles and politics into approved ends of power. In such periods, popular memory is appropriated to support the facade of normalcy for the present. The political nostalgist has us behold a fictional past and urges us to be like him and become what we behold.

Such a nostalgic universe is an image of a stable social hierarchy that never existed but should. But for a vulnerable people threatened by no sense of place in the here and now, an imaginary past is preferable to none at all and certainly to a critical past of harsh events and uncertain processes. The nostalgic impulse transforms the past into a romantic drama wherein the institutions of the stable social hierarchy are created and placed. It is an aesthetic universe that exists in time, a "cliotopia" that dwells in an inaccessible elsewhere of the Land of Back. The past is an aesthetic dream-sanctuary wherein heroism serves the cause of democratic order. Nostalgia conjures a vision of democracy, both beyond and on human scale. Through the primal experience of the nostalgic ritualist, the ghosts of time past become the conjured spirits that resanctify the present.

The Magical Origins of Kings

Ronald Reagan identified himself with the innocent power of the prelapsarian world. In a sense, his entire political career was autobiographical, based on getting audiences to share the image of him as a representation of the perpetual experience the popular mind associates with that world. His identification with both the myth of the West and the myth of the Town combined two powerful images. He conveyed the impression of being both sheriff and mayor, a Western domestic that would provide both defense against evil intrusion and benevolent rule of the peaceable kingdom. Both the ranch in the California hills and the house in Dixon stood as monuments to the self-defined myth of magical origins. Both were symbolic locations that could associate him with the principled violence of the Western folktale and the domestic tranquility of the small town of yore. Reagan could be only tangentially self-associated with mythic times such as World War II, but he was successfully self-placed in a key moment of the creation of modern America, the time when the vitality of frontier barbarism is tamed and put to work building the institutional order of local self-government. That the facts of Reagan's early life do not fit the representation is of little moment; what is important is that he evoked, and many apparently accepted, the image of himself as the latest, and perhaps the last, embodiment of primal and perpetual experience that should inform and re-enchant the present. The mythic moment of Reagan's magical origins was the creation of popular civilization, the age of the ascendancy of bourgeois normalcy. Reagan represented himself as an agent of popular civilization who combined in his personage the unity of etiology and identity, familiarity with the origins of local self-government from which logically flowed the model personality of popular male heroes such as he. Reagan was a recognizable democratic hero, resembling the popular tradition of the hero who led the many not through his superiority as much as through his commonality. Heroism is a property of the popularity of the local innocent trustworthy as one of us. Reagan was not a hero from a Vicoian age of the gods (such as the Founding Fathers) or age of natural aristocracy (the captains of industry and invention such as Ford or Edison), but rather was of a popular age, the time of the creation of the popular order.

The Town, then, exists at the *axis mundi* of popular history, the time and place of the establishment of popular mythography. The Town is memorable as a metaphor of human scale, a symbolic place in the *terra incognita* of the American interior, contrastable with the untamed Frontier from which it drew its institutional and heroic vitality but also from the cosmopolitan and cynical City. In that sense, it is always a "Middletown" and Our Town, the true placement of romantic democracy. But the Town has more than elegiac function. It is a model of the logic of a popular society, an institutional order that locates self-government in its proper place and scale. In the American search for the right locale, this is the place. As an agent of popular civilization, Ronald Reagan could uncomplicate the world through his access to the popular omniscience inherent in such a cultural referent. In the town, there truly were simple solutions for every problem. Reagan could apply the logic of a popular society to the contemporary world found wanting of the common sense of accessible popular knowledge at work in the meta-historical order.

Such an evocation is not a celebration of archaism, but an earnest hope that somehow the celebration of an earlier and primal metaphor can overcome the terror of history. Reagan's association with the primal unit of nostalgic culture gave him the power of self-placement. He claimed to have magical origins which gave him access to the fundamental mystery of the primal American locale. He understood the logic of popular order as it once existed and should still exist. His own etiology made him the identifiable model American Self, who in both thought and being represented the elementary ideas and conduct of the promised national life. Reagan's public self was for a time the very theater of politico-cultural drama, whereby his private imagination of his origins and destiny became identified with ours. His application of the "lessons of the past" to the present was more of a stance than a program, a judgment than an ideology. This is not to suggest that Reagan did not have ideas about using the past to help shape the future. Quite the contrary, his imagination of the moral and material superiority of the locally self-governing Town suggested the paradoxical position of prospective atavism, which would use the mysterious knowledge of an earlier and primitive age and place not to revert to then, but rather to make the present unfolding time reacquire some of the romantic enchantment and beauty lost in the mistake of time and circumstance. The impulse of Reaganism was therefore not so much "conservative" or even "reactionary" as it was nativistic and as nostalgic about the future as the past. The meaning of Ronald Reagan has less to do with social issues and more to do about national folktales.

Referring to Reagan's autobiography, *Where's the Rest of Me?*, Gregg Easterbrook points out that Reagan's account of his own life imitates art, requiring a willing suspension of disbelief on the part of the reader, and by extension, the voter. His life story as told is just too good to be true—there are no really bad times, all anecdotes have a happy ending, luck always intervenes at the right moment for things to work out, life is an uninterrupted and easy climb to the top, happy endings are in the dramatic nature of things, or as Reagan wrote for his high school senior yearbook, "Life is just one grand sweet song, so start the music." This vision of life is deeply rooted in the myth of the good community, and our nostalgic consciousness of it has real political consequences:

Dismissing the existence of bad times means more than the desire to rearrange the past into a pleasant haze. It means more than restorationist nostalgia for the good old days, a standby of politics and a longing that tugs on us all, to one degree or another. It means the desire to see the world *literally the way Rockwell saw it*, a powerful element of the Republican soul. In Rockwell's art bad luck and injustice are not depicted; *therefore, they do not exist*. Rockwell will deal with an unpleasant subject, but only with its most polite and presentable manifestations. (Easterbrook 17)

By extension, the Rockwell vision is a popular representation that explains much of why we are trying to run a large empire on the image of a small town, indeed on values and practices that are more the province of our popular imagination than the realities of earlier small town life. But the Rockwell image persists as a nostalgic model of an organic community of families, friends and neighbors, and benevolent institutions, an harmonious unit of local self-government that enjoys the moral and material fruits of the American Dream. It omits from consciousness social problems and disagreeable social groups (classes of poor, minorities, intellectuals). And it has difficulty dealing with proposals and trends which violate the popular ideal, including the intervention of the national government to enforce its will.

This popular image is a powerful source of what Vidich and Bensman called "the public ideology" at the local level, reinforcing consensus of the universal validity of the values of the classic small town, reinforced by the sentimental rhetoric of believers from local Chambers of Commerce up to Reagan. Vidich and Bensman also noted something else: that the rhetoric of the public ideology was ritual, empty of meaning and relevance, but that the will to believe was so strong that the believers in the town had mastered a kind of Orwellian doublethink. Rituals of mutual reinforcement of the semi-official public ideology were the subject of polite talk:

...[T]he social mores of the small town at every opportunity demand that only those facts and ideas which support the dreamwork of everyday life are to be verbalized and selected out for emphasis and repetition. Those who disbelieve the public ideology typically remain silent, since discouraging words are a threat to the system of illusion even though many persons do not in an inner way hold to its tenets. (Vidich and Bensman)

The Reagan phenomenon stems from his rootedness in the classic small town of popular fantasy, his representation to the national community of the public ideology that undergirded it and the mass desire for simple reaffirmation of values—and the enchanted place they were once manifest—threatened by the impersonal tides of history. The etiology of the political culture reveals the "true" American identity, represented and writ large in the national public life by an exponent of the world of illusion. Since the American identity is now Protean in its choice of multiple selves, Reagan's illusion that his Rockwellville roots and populist homestyle appealed to those who sought stable identity, a moral self that would not founder on the rocks.

Norman Rockwell said that "I paint life as I would like it to be." Like Rockwell, Reagan was a popular artist of the American Dream, as located in the Town. Rockwell had made the American Dream into concrete images of romantic democracy—the hopes and joys of youth, the bonds of family and friendship, the wisdom of age, the justice of local institutions, the heritage of the "four freedoms" as seen in town meetings in school rooms, children safely sleeping, prayer in the churches of our choice, a family united over Thanksgiving bounty. Reagan celebrated in his autobiographical self-representation the reality and virtue of such a dreamworld, the insubstantial mythography of the metaphorical enchanted location.

He penned the preface to a collection of Rockwell's illustrations, including a testament of relevance: the country had changed since the era Rockwell portrayed, he said, "yet the values that he cherished and celebrated—love of God and country, hard work, neighborhood, and family—still give us strength, and will shape our dreams for decades to come" (ix). Reagan was one who did shape our dreams during his ascendancy through the use of Rockwellian cultural referents. His public memories of boyhood are transformed into a "Huck Finn-Tom Sawyer idyll" and the simple gifts of small-town life. Even if, as his biographical critics insist, it has little actual validity, the fact that many were willing and able to share the fantasy attests to its remarkable salience at this late date in American history. The pastoral, after all, is an indelible part of American nostalgia, and small-town pastoralism remains as the bastion of grassroots wisdom and virtue. Reagan evoked his own mythic familiarity with what the Town still represents: the loss of community.

This is the significance, however constrained, of "Ronald Reagan's Boyhood Home" in Dixon, Illinois. The Reagan family lived there from 1920 to 1923 as renters. It was refurbished to resemble a home typical in the prelapsarian community and opened by Reagan himself during the 1984 campaign visit. Like all such shrines, it serves the symbolic function of placing the myth of community in an edifice where the hero learned the wisdom and virtue that was later to make him great. The creation of such a place obviously serves propaganda purposes, although no more cynically than another shrine of heroic origin. We have every reason to believe that Reagan painted life as he would like it to be, and we certainly have evidence that many wished to share the mystery of the romantic community lost and refound. The Reagan coalition was less political than it was mythological. It was founded less in a will to power and more in a will to believe. If the recurrent impulse is to renormalize a new, and ever more remote, world, it is not only because so many Americans cannot tolerate random and recalcitrant new realities, but also because at each juncture the myth of the romantic community seems all the more irrecoverable or even irrelevant. But the will to believe in original innocence is great and converges on representations such as Reagan and the house in Dixon. Of the many houses built and destroyed in the axial period of the twentieth century, this comes to be one that acquires the sacral status of shrine, a monument to the will to believe in the magical origins of kings. The "Boyhood Home" acquired official status in 1982 by inclusion in the National Register of Historical Places (although in the 1920s the Reagan family lived in four other houses in Dixon alone) and is owned by the appropriately titled "Ronald Reagan Home Preservation Foundation." Like Reagan himself, the "boyhood home" enshrines the myth of his idyllic past and charmed life; that the house represents how the kind of local foundation where the right values and attitudes were taught and imbibed; and that the house symbolized the American local "home" that is our once and future democratic castle.

The house in Dixon, then, is a symbol of the microcosmic familial unit of the Town, the institution from which local self-government arises and the primal bond from which Presidential omniscience of popular will and society originates. It has been suggested that Americans in the electronic age have lost their "sense of place," including a vacuous absence of ability to give meaning to contemporary social locations such as shrines and inhabitations (Meyrowitz). The lack of a sense of place in the here and now, however, does not mean that people do not desire, nor are able to imagine, the kind of place represented by the "Boyhood Home" in Dixon. Indeed, the feeling of displacement in history threatens to give credence to the terrifying feeling of existential ahistoricity. The complex of emotional connotations the house in Dixon evokes are folk memories that are not a part of our lived experience but certainly are a part of our appropriated memories. Such evocations made Reagan to be for politics what Rockwell was to art. Both were popular artists who were able to make our dreams of a romantic state visible. Both painted the American Dream as something that existed in a place of imaginative unity and humanity. It is a dream-state, to be sure; but it is not their private fanciful past. Rather it is ours, and their gift was to give aesthetic form to a devoutly desired metahistorical pretense.

Reagan's evocation of the lost world of Dixon, from ice cream socials to barnraisings, offers us an irresistible spectacle of a community that possesses in our minds mythic adequacy. The Town has the institutional and role structure that sustains our will to believe in an imaginary state and associate Reagan as someone qualified to run that state. The Town is a metaphor of popular idealism, a place where the majestic folklore of romantic democracy unfolds in magical narratives that vindicate the logic of a popular society. It is a place of natural wisdom, of caring mothers and hardworking and faithful fathers, kindly country doctors, crusty but benign judges, crusading newspaper editors, tolerant but firm sheriffs, simple but wise servants, ministers who provide gentle spiritual guidance, teachers who care for their pupils, even whores with a gold heart.

The Town is the symbolic place where the romantic story of the origins and rise to greatness of democratic kings begins. It is the place to start the narrative of the Presidential folk monomyth, be it New Salem, Galena, Marion, Abilene, or Plains. Way back home is the place to be from, and never forget your humble origins and rootedness in the essential goodness of the community. Those who leave the Town to achieve share the ideals of the community and serve as metaphors of popular mobility who are so because of what they learned back home. They go out in the world emboldened with the myth that they can run large economic or political empires on the model of a small town remote from the centers of power. But since democratic kings must enact a majestic folktale that starts with their magical origins, the Town serves as a point of mythic departure from which the hero's quest is undertaken. The hero carries the values of the Town with him (and in some cases, her) and in a sense never leaves: he governs the corporation or the capital with a home style that forever links him with his roots and makes him away from home a bemused outsider who straightens out the unholy mess in Sacramento or Washington or even Moscow by the power of his cultural referent. Reagan could apply the primitive model of village heroism against the labyrinths of cosmopolitan power, pitting the logic of popular society to defeat the alien pretensions and errors of political establishments.

The Town hero who conquers the world, then, is a public being who triumphs over adversity in the world through his metapolitical status and orientation. Reagan's defense of the realm was not a defense of government. Rather he defended the realm of local self-government as it was intended to be, the logic of "the proper functions" of government. The local model of harmonic institutional order was supposed to govern the operation of government at all levels, not the other way around. Reagan's conception of government was romantic both in its intentions and conduct. Government was severely circumscribed in some ways by the legitimate provinces of other local institutions—family, church, business. On the other hand, it was supposed to be heroic in its defense of town and country from alien and promotion of moral and material prosperity within the peaceable kingdom. In the romance of community for the grass-roots mind, government serves selective and contradictory functions, interfering with individual and institutional freedom in some areas but not in others. The American popular romantic envisions a harmonic state of consensus on virtue and freedom, with government governed itself by the essential goodness and common sense that comprises the Town.

We get some sense of how rooted the American folktale is in the grass-roots mind by examining young Reagan's reading. The popular books he once told a librarian had influenced him the most are popular romances about heroic achievement by ordinary but ambitious and vigorous youths. One book, *That Printer of Udell* by Harold Bell Wright, is an Alger-like tale of a youth on the road looking for work. Young Dick Falken goes to night school to improve himself and indeed shows his worth by solving a murder, saving a pretty socialite from life in a brothel (and then marries her) and finally is elected to Congress "to enter a life of wider usefulness at the National Capitol." The young hero sees that the small town community doesn't follow Christ's teachings and applies "civic Christianity" and "municipal virtues" to the conduct of business and government. The power of this hybrid of boosterism and religiosity to transform the community is remarkable. Led by energetic Dick Falken, the town is transformed into a kind of Midwestern Utopia in which people "were struck by good, common-sense business Christianity." Saloons are replaced by business firms; thieves and prostitutes find work; burlesque houses are replaced by musical and lecture pavilions; churches flourish, school attendance grows and streets and laws are well-kept. Social welfare—which is private and voluntary—includes an "Institute for Helping the Unemployed" that helps those willing to work but excludes the undeserving.

Other books on Reagan's list included Westerns, Edgar Rice Burroughs novels about Tarzan, the Ape Man and John Carter, Warlord of Mars, a Frank Merriwell at Yale novel and King Arthur. The Merriwell novel "inspired him to play football once he had decided to become a Frank Merriwell." Reagan could identify himself with such a character easily enough. Indeed, Merriwell creator Gilbert Patten saw that fictional figure as an exemplar of the best features of the American male character, someone "frank for frankness, merry for a happy disposition, well for health and abundant vitality." Merriwell is a born leader in the democratic competition and cooperation of sports, "none of his friends was ever a sneak, cheapskate, or a sissy," and he himself was "a shining light for every ambitious lad to follow." Reagan, in his letter to the librarian, characterized these formative books as "thrilling but wholesome entertainment that endorsed many of the older values that the post-war world would now disparage: individualism, a healthy self-reliance, chastity, woman as help-mate to man, hardship as moral-builder." He admitted their influence by concluding, "All in all, as I look back I realize that all my reading left an abiding belief in the triumph of good over evil. There were heroes who lived by standards of morality and fair play." And: "I'm a sucker for hero-worship to this day" (Griswold 11).

Reagan's own heroic origin and rise is as much an ahistorical fiction as the folktales of Dick Falken and Frank Merriwell, but it has solid mythological standing. For the myth of the magical origins and quest of the hero is a virtually universal folktale and was quickly applied to the Presidency with Washington. Even with considerable evidence that Reagan invented much of the narrative of his charmed past and fated climb to glory, people were as willing as he to suspend disbelief and worship a hero of his own making. Indeed, the fact that it was an aesthetic recreation made it all the more compelling in an incoherent and vulnerable present. For Reagan, it was a successful psychological and political exercise in heroic self-enchantment, the transformation of personal history into a mythic narrative and personal anecdotes into representative didactics. For those who found the pretense enchanting, it was an act of apochryphal play that shared the old fantasy of a hero with the mantle of mythic adequacy. The public complicity, or acquiescence, involved the featuring of an archaic cultural foreknowledge that took precedence over immediate and palpable concerns or deprivations.

The re-enchanted metauniverse that Reagan willed gave him a kind of mortal splendor in the present. This quality made him seem both old and young: old in the sense of being a venerable citizen of the Town, and forever young as the spiritual carrier of what the Town represents.

Reagan was able as few before him to imbue the Presidency with a remarkable combination of human and epic scale. The Town is the nostalgic mythography of popular covenant conceived at the axial moment of romantic democracy. The covenant had the blessing of God and the national democratic faith, and now even if it cannot be fully regained it can be identified through the last of those who knew it. If popular narratives are fables of identity about paradise lost and regained, this American fable suffers from the paradox of nostalgia. When high school students applauded Reagan for invoking the spirit of barnraising, and when he remarked that every child should grow up in a small town just as he did, it involved no expectation that this world would someday magically reappear, nor support for a draconian agenda of enforced restoration. But since now the future isn't what it used to be, then the only other alternative is believing that the past was what Reagan claimed it used to be. If the present involves the terror of the loss of covenant, it is gratifying that the past can be redeemed even if the future cannot be saved.

The paradox of nostalgia is that it recreates an unusable past that serves only as a statement of faith and not of learning. Indeed, the politics of nostalgia asks for historical unlearning, suggesting not a wiser but rather a childish innocence. The popular covenant of the Town is a pact with youth and not maturity. The Town was the epic journey's end of the American quest, a domestic epic of the establishment of perfect symmetry. But such a completion of the human popular order suggests that everything that comes after is burdened with the corruption of time. The nostalgic politician can only succeed at a time in which there is a need for nostalgia. Such times must by definition suffer by comparison with the prelapsarian and must be a period of political drift and exhaustion in which the uncorrupted agent of the popular covenant of yore succeeds precisely because there is a vacuum that the fall from grace has created. Reagan's covenant was with the past and not the future. Nostalgia expresses confidence in the past but not the future.

At an early age, then, Reagan was able to identify with the domestic heroism of nostalgic democracy, the metaphor of the townscape as the theater of popular action that serves the common weal. Reagan was the image of the boy mayor of Rockwell, the American version of the widespread folktale of the child-king who rules the kingdom through the innocence of provincial idealism. The Town is the ideal "middle landscape" of the past that offered the boy mayor command of the universe of normalcy. However variously it was conceived—Walnut Grove, Hannibal, Lake Wobegon, Greenwillow, Grover's Corner s—rule was conducted through the popular genius of the ingenuous hero. The local state of perfect order was ruled by magic, not power. The boy mayor's strength was in popularity, not cunning. The harmonic democracy of the Town was self-ruled and only needed public government to be reminded through the good offices of domestic leadership espousing the potency of belief and example. Reagan brought to national politics the orthodoxies and orthopraxies of local democracy, expressed as the "practical idealism" of boy mayorship turned President.

There are many examples of this stance, but no better one than the practice of unilateral domestic interventionism. The fundamental social premise of Rockwell is that there are no sociological categories or problems. The Town is a community of discrete individuals for whom there is occasional trouble or bad luck. But since the Town is classless and compassionate, it is the role of the boy mayor to alert the citizenry to individual difficulties, or to quietly resolve the individual problem through private action. The principle also extends to the recognition of achievement and service. Thus Reagan would recognize individual heroes of private initiative or lifesaving in a State of the Union address, call athletes or teams that had just triumphed and call for organ transplants and donations for sick children. For the little girl in Texas who was caught in a well, her rescue brought a call to the parents and the expression that the nation had become her "godfathers" and "godmothers." Reagan was the Town-nation leader of popular omnipotence, expressing care and concern as if it were a phenomenon specific to a small group. In Rockwell, there is only personal and not political compassion, since the latter admits of classes and categories of the deprived and wronged and would legitimate the demand for welfare programs and class conflict. Expressions of personal compassion by the boy mayor-President— reading a letter in a speech from a worried grandmother—personalize politics, and by so doing suggests that personal intervention in unilateral domestic situations is sufficient, and therefore negates the necessity or utility of official government programs. The principle extends to a host of public functions Reagan thought illegitimate—day care, equal opportunity, affirmative action and so on. It reached its most remarkable fruition in the personal expressions by the Reagans about drugs, including the hand-holding "Just Say NO" speech while at the very moment his Administration was drastically cutting public funds for anti-drug programs.

Reagan's authority, then, stemmed from his self-association with magical origins and quest for self-fulfillment in an adult role as leader of the national village. In his case the hero's quest originates in a primal scene, and in a sense it is a place he never leaves. Reagan emerged as a popular authority, a personage whose authority was above ordinary authority. He could run against government on a national scale as the bearer of the popular omniscience of local self-government. He bore the knowledge of a sentimental journey not to the past but rather to the present. But it made his political relationship to the present over which he presided a metaphorical one: he ruled and imaginary state, government as it was meant to be in the metachronic world from which he drew his authority. He ruled a locale of perfect symmetry firsthand, and only in a derivative sense as a bemused outsider did he rule the national state. It made him forever unresponsible for what government as an alien leviathan, and forever responsive to the nostalgia for the true government of the middle and archaic townscape of the Town. His identification with the imaginary state of popular mythography allowed him to preside over a fallen national state for which he was not responsible. Reagan governed a romance, not a reality. Therefore he could rail against deficits or welfare or bureaucracy while "on watch" as President. In an important sense, he defined the role as head of state rather than head of government, correctly assessing the scope of his authority.

Reagan's relationship with the political present of the 1980s was in essence metaphorical. He was an analogical figure of innocence beyond the ordinary frustrations of actual politics. Having posited that he drew his sustenance from the symmetrical cosmology of the Town, the contemporary world had then to adapt to him. He carried the elemental fire of prelapsarian truth, uncorrupted and pristine, into the present without fear of the corrosive force of time nor the failure of the application of principle.

Reagan's origins in the Town made his values generic. No matter how derivative temporal politics might become, as a statement of faith he offered us a vision of original community and as a statement of nostalgic vindication the opportunity to celebrate through him the rectitude of genesis. Reagan's progress was from romance to ritual: putative origins in the metaphorical community translated into ritual celebration in the palace of the hero's quest. But the completion of the quest did not mandate a draconian agenda to restore the symmetry of the Town. Rather it dictated ritual obeisance to the romance of popular memory, as represented by the boy mayor as President who came from the beginning of time.

The Shape of Popular Memory

In his first Inaugural Address, Reagan urged that "we have every right to dream heroic dreams." We have argued here that this vision of popular order is nostalgic, offering a grass-roots folk model of local self-government and bourgeois normalcy that served Reagan's purposes of romantic nationalism and the perpetuation of the American Dream. To reassert belief in "our capacity to perform great deeds" harkened us back not to the great deeds of corporate or political empire, but to the democratic heroism of ordinary life ("You can see heroes every day going in and out of factory gates"). We located the domestic epic in the mythopoetic setting of the small town, but with the hero's quest representing the integrity, and only limited applicability, of the innocent world against the accumulation of historical experience. Reagan was a spokesman for the invincibility of American innocence in defiance of pragmatic rule, as imagined in our popular memory of an atemporal moment of enchanted community. It may have been a created reality that was an exercise in political solipsism, but it was a solipsism that we shared. Reagan's political self-enchantment was an exercise in "foreverthink," someone conversant with the mnemonic spectacle of romantic democracy, a time both past and forever.

The worship of the Town and what it represents for our belief in domestic heroism does belie a fundamental preference for sometime else than in the present. But it is easier to prefer the romantic locale created by classical Hollywood (and other forms of popular media), since it was a reality that could be commanded. Like the Main Street at Disneyland, the charm and tenacity of the back lot Rockwells perpetuated the imagination of a place of pristine identity. Reagan's elegiac reminiscences about lost Hollywood had undertones of Hollywood as the fulfillment of the promise of the Town: eternal summer, tribal health and beauty, commercial harmony, the celebration of bourgeois values, the happy place of MGM's famous Sunday picnics presided over by benevolent capitalists. Not only did Hollywood enshrine Dixon on film, Hollywood itself has something of the identity of place that the rest of America was so rapidly losing. For Reagan and so many Americans like him, Hollywood offered a sense of belonging to a state of grace that had the permanence of cinemaphotogenic repeatability. It has the magical power to recreate the tree-lined street, the general store, the soda fountain, the friends and neighbors of folkish culture. And Hollywood itself could serve as a latter-day model for a reformed Town of technological normalcy, as with the 1950s Reagans living in a futuristic General Electric home and the 1980s Reagans extolling the conspicuous consumption of Beverly Hills. Reagan's American Dream would somehow combine Rockwell and Hollywood in a unified romantic world.

Yet the impact of such a vision on policy was minimal, since it was experienced and shared as play. Both Rockwell and Hollywood were second-order realities of normative structure immune from the asychronic spasms of history, places that we know and love precisely because they are so unlike our immediate and palpable life. Reagan's America was populated by reality malcontents who shared an imaginative spectacle of a platonic and not a pragmatic world. But nostalgia for the non-existent belies a certain poignant sense of irrevocable loss, a process that has been termed "the falsification of memory" (Vidich and Bensman 302-304). Whether this suggests a widespread social pathology stemming from historical dislocation is an open question, but it does surely demonstrate the current bankruptcy, or perhaps inferior status, of the actual. To accord a figure like Reagan the mythic status of magical origins may strike the Machiavellian realist as romantic nonsense, but it was part of the Reagan mystique that captured, or perhaps revived, the national folkish imagination. His representation of the myth of the Town involved not only the recrudescence of mythic politics, but also more deeply the success of popular culture in perpetuating play with the past that translates at the Presidential level at least into political power. Reagan's grip on us was surest when he self-associated, through such symbolic acts as the trip to Dixon, with romantic democracy, and most clumsy when he committed the profanation of descent from the ludenic to the pragmatic. In an important sense, Reagan was a confidence man, whose task was to use the resources of popular memory in order to restore confidence in the sacral status of government. The re-enactment of mythic associations like the house in Dixon were rituals of confidence, demonstrating that his self-confidence in his own origins and destiny, the completion of his quest for "the rest of me," gave him the metaphorical transcendence to be an exemplar of confidence.

But the Rockwellian vision of commercial and political nostalgia is incomplete. Our confidence in the popular order of the Town as exemplified by the Boy Mayor was complemented, and often threatened to be undermined, by a darker vision. The model world of Rockwell suffers from excessive optimism and puerility, denying the puritan strain of belief in sin. Reagan's worldview omitted original sin and, indeed, the need for suffering and sacrifice to achieve salvation. The Town was already saved by national and not spiritual grace. Hollywood itself could never resist exploiting the belief that beneath the facade of official harmony and respectability lurk all dark urges of the puritan imagination, nor deny the spectacular immorality that surfaced in the movie capital. Hollywood catered to that competing image, what we may call the Gothic Town. Reagan's own favorite film, *King's Row*, is a Gothic vision of Dixon whose underlying evil punishes and nearly destroys the confident and facile Reagan (Drake McHugh) character, someone who would make a nice Boy Mayor in happier circumstances. Similarly, Reagan was an admirer of the 1930s films of Frank Capra, who gave vigorous tribute to the vision of popular order and the democratic hero who overcame elite forces to demonstrate the magic of the national faith. (Reagan quoted the Gary Cooper radio speech in *Meet John Doe* early in his first term and planned on, but then dropped, making a reference to "fighting for lost causes" from *Mr. Smith Goes to Washington* during the Bork nomination fight.) Yet Capra's penultimate vision of the town, in *It's a Wonderful Life*, is a Gothic tale of dark motives, repressed desires and social failure, a place beset by class exploitation, sinister capitalism, marital entrapment, familial betrayal and frustrated ambitions. The famous nighttown sequence of George Bailey's tour of "Pottersville" simply shows the Town devoid of the pretenses of daylight, its own evil carried to its logical conclusion rather than to the popular logic of Rockwell. It took divine intervention (and Capra's usual *deus ex machina*) to prevent the conscience and de facto Boy Mayor of the community from committing suicide, and rather sustaining a Christmas hope just one day longer. But Bedford Falls, even at the end, will never be a Rockwell, nor Bailey a confident Boy Mayor; if he redeems the community at last, it will be as a suffering servant ruling an Augustinian Town, always on the brink of the abyss.

Such Gothic tales of the Town had contrived "happy" endings, giving some displaced satisfaction that all was well in the realm of imaginative longings. But it is a clue as to how disturbing such recurrent images are that Reagan denied them. There were no snakes in his vision of the Town, and the people of the village were sinned against but did not themselves sin. To admit the validity of the Gothic Town would constitute a denial of the sunny mythology with which he self-associated. Bleak or hopeless images of the recent American past threatened the recrudescence of historical representation. Bedford Falls was supposed to remain the same as it ever was at least through the last prelapsarian age of popular memory, the 1950s. Reagan, after all, came to political prominence as a cultural spokesman for the Eisenhower normalcy of the extended era of the 1950s, celebrated in the family situation-comedies of 1950s television. Reagan appeared in the present of the fallen 1980s as a representative of the reformed Rockwell of the 1950s, a model of assured affluence and cultural continuity. He had come to political power as a reaction against the reforms and innovations of the 1960s and as spokesman for a coalition that won the Presidency in the wake of the pessimism and exhaustion of the 1970s. The playful hope of prospective atavism he represented was tellingly captured in the film *Back to the Future* (1985). The young protagonist vows in the awful present that "history is going to change," in the face of the alien threat of Libyan terrorists and the domestic threat of community and familial decay. He returns to 1955, reforms his soon-to-be-parents and joins in the innocent joys of prelapsarian communal life. The past is revised into the romantic fantasy of nostalgic community, and the cowardly father-to-be is saved from emasculation through the use of violence. The young time traveler returns to a personally redeemed and prosperous family, a perfect privatistic model of a 1980s family without historical memory of social consciousness and a Town that is just as decayed. Prospective atavism offers no hope of political redemption, only the assertion that the reformed 1950s familial unit suggests a personal model for survival and prosperity in a present Town that cannot be saved and should indeed be evaded through personal ambition and consumption. Reagan's promise, in that way, was that only the personal and not the political past was relevant to the present and offered himself as a personal paragon who had forgotten or denied the all-too-real recent past, and that there were, in short, historical limits to what the Boy Mayor of the Town could do other than represent himself in a kind of political epiphany that did not change history, but for which history had changed.

Reagan's nostalgic association with the leadership of the mythic Town was consistent with the American tradition that politics is to be understood in the development of self, and further that he could offer his representative self as a metaphor of transcending the present. It made him someone who was in his Presidential time, but not of it. He could not redeem the present, but he could represent the past. He could not conquer temporality, but he could eulogize eternity. He could not change recent history, but he could discredit it. He could not stop the decline in the belief in future progress, but he could celebrate reverence for the idea of progress vested in the metahistory of the Town. Both the values and the integrity of the small town had by the 1980s become a political anachronism, but we responded to Reagan's twilight bravado as a symbol of continuity, identity, or hope even if in our moments of existential self-awareness we knew it all to be an aesthetic creation, a nostalgic thing of beauty that was a joy forever. The Town was part of an unusable past that remained, through Reagan's representation of it, an indelible image of what we still seemed to think that we were and could have been. If we felt that now history and our own fate were out of control, we at least had the comfort of remembering that sunny place where the ludenic hero of our time once strode and from which he descended to remind us of the pride of mythic place.

Chapter Two
The Family

In the Rockwellian moment of the Town, the primal institution of the imaginary state is the family. In the popular imagination, it is sometimes the rural extended family such as the Waltons or the nuclear families of either archaic Dixons or reformed suburban Ozzie and Harriet Nelson households. But in all cases the impulse is derived from a growing contemporary sense of the passage of familial normalcy. The family had been part of the mythic high ground of Rockwell, the sacral unit of social order and the metaphorical microcosm of the political myth that America constitutes a large family that shares values and habits as represented by a Presidential First Family headed by a First Father (or perhaps First Uncle). Both the families of popular culture and the First Family of the popular Presidency had been preceded by the folk myth of the happy and harmonious family home, and indeed by the myth of the hearth under siege. Alien threats from Indian kidnappings to Communist subversion always had the destruction of the family as their demonic agenda, and domestic threats from the lure of the new cities to teenage drugs all served as evidence of the dangerous temporal descent from the perfect symmetry of the family to its destruction or transformation. We may doubt that such perfection ever existed, since the American family has always been pressured by centrifugal forces, but we still appreciate the atemporal myth. We appreciate it all the more at a time when those centrifugal forces seem triumphant, and when the primary influences in our lives are from sources other than the family.

The house in Dixon, in that case, was a popular home, a place where the prototypical family of prelapsarian America could have resided. Reagan could claim popular knowledge of this primal scene and ground political heroism in the charming ordinariness of that original reminiscence—the virtues of the acts of moral courage (refusing to let children see *The Birth of a Nation*), private thus legitimate charity, the adventures with friends, the dear hearts and gentle people in the safe and solid houses on tree-lined streets in soft summer nights. The nostalgic image of The Family suggests a clear hierarchical role structure, with that primal unit serving as a microcosmic model for the larger society and subsequent times such as the 1980s. The politics of nostalgia uses the Family as a metaphor of domestic power, one that instructs us in a social hierarchy headed by older adult males in positions of social power, complemented by women in supporting if vital roles as help meet and carrier of the feminine virtues of civilization and domestic peace, and obeyed by those deemed children in whatever sense, including the underage, servants and the socially irresponsible. If the story of early Reagan was a folktale, it was a fable of power, a ritual retelling of who should have power in a stable social hierarchy justified by magical origins in romantic democracy.

The house in Dixon, and the image of the Family that it symbolizes, became in enshrinement something of a talisman, a place to be retouched because of the political truth it represents. A "pro-family" stance is rooted in mythological and not philosophical foundations, known by the Boy Mayor walking down tree-lined Elm Street and not by dreary academic tomes. Symbolic Home and Family, then, serve the political function of iconological didacticism, teaching us once again the truths inherent in the simple white frame house and the "heap o'living" that in the popular imagination made that house a home. And it taught us not only the mythic superiority of the original Town and Home from which we have strayed. The Reagan's tour of the restored First House reminded us that no matter how far in the world they have soared, they could still touch down and pay homage to the humble origins they still venerated and ostensibly carried even to Hollywood and Washington. Posing at the Dixon home, the Reagans were cultural icons, First Father and Mother, who would instruct us that familial authorities still clung to the solid foundational frame of popular order. For Ronald Reagan, the house in Dixon was the historical edifice of the First of Him, giving the youthful impetus to the hero's quest that would let us discover and enjoy the Rest of Him. The Reagans were transformed, through the alchemy of popular imagination, into political archetypes, figures who served as metaphors of familial identity at a time when that institution was taking pluralistic form. A familial archetype suggests a monomythic role structure, with the provinces of power and authority clearly defined. Ronald Reagan was a nostalgic archetype of male power, and Nancy Reagan was a nostalgic archetype of female power.

The Archetype of Male Power

The logic of a popular society is based not so much on the rational formulations of forensic articulation as it is in the cultural imagination of mythic models. But the institutional alliance of The Town has to be represented by heroic figures who "man" and "woman" those sacral habits. The *axis mundi* of American civilization was created out of violence against aliens, foreign and then indigenous. The founding myth required iconic archetypes of male power, figures capable of the kind of decisive action necessary to create the conditions of civilization, and then to man the institutions created. The most popular folktale celebrating the founding has been the classical Western, a democratic tale about how the West was won and what came of it. The asocial hero possessed of a kind of savage charisma acts to create order out of chaos, even though he cannot be part of what he creates. He is part of chaos, the wilderness that lies beyond, leaving the legacy of a new sacred order and also the legitimacy of exceptional violence with the subsequent appearance of an alien threat. In this popular tradition, the violent hero of yore is an outsider who can never be part of the responsibilities of The Town. He conquers chaos to create a democratic order; his lesson to those who man the institutions created is to not only run them well but also to defend them from alien threat.

The popular icon of the Western hero, from Natty Bumppo down through the screen characters of John Wayne and Clint Eastwood, remains an ideal of male independence as a prerequisite for effective action. But the lesson of this asocial and violent figure alone is potentially anarchic. Thus the torch of power is passed with the founding of civilization to those men who will make their compromise with society and exercise peaceful power within its orderly confines and collective violent power only against those aliens who would threaten it. Perhaps the most poignant treatment of this in the movies is John Ford's *The Man Who Shot Liberty Valance* (1962), in which John Wayne, the archetype of the lone frontiersman, actually kills the wild and destructive Valance, but with meaningful irony, the credit goes to the archetype of the civilized social leader, James Stewart, symbolizing both the anachronism of anarchic individualism, good or bad, and the investiture of social power in males who will rule The Town and if need be now exercise the option of violent defense against aggression.

Civilized males, then, would rule the institutions of romantic democracy, making the compromises symbolized by Andrew Jackson for the purpose of social order and progress. But the heritage and interplay of heroic archetypes suggests a duality, even a dilemma, in the American male character. For the icon of figures such as Wayne idealizes male autonomy and self-reliance, an independence from society and its rules. The Man of the West occupies an imaginary state of nature and possesses a charismatic power derived from his experience as a child of nature. Indeed, his is the only American charisma that is truly undiluted by social compromise: his "gift of grace" is derived from nature, not society, and cannot be compromised or routinized by his acceptance of permanent social leadership in The Town. But charismatic authority is a feature of the leadership of movement such as the founding of civilizations. It is therefore a threat to the institutional alliance of society if it is not diluted into social popularity and diminished enthusiasm. The Wayne-figure is charismatic but unsociable, potentially a threat to regular churchgoing, garden clubs and banks; the Stewart-figure is uncharismatic but sociable, the boy-mayor who coordinates the institutional alliance.

Reagan's identification with the myth of the West, and himself as a Man of the West, was both political advantage and burden for him. He could represent himself as a Westerner independent of the institutional constraints of Capital City and thus be able to take the decisive action necessary to secure the treasury and fight off alien threats. The affection of things Western served to reinforce the image. He could make a claim to possess the charisma of nature and to infuse society again with a renewed spirit of rugged individualism. He could argue that he understood the necessity of the Western ethic of violent solutions to alien threats. It associated him with the mythic identity of an archetypical male role deeply rooted in American history. As he came to power, the revival of this ur-figure allowed us to engage in fantasies of American male ascendancy—over assertive women, androgynous men, the restraints of social order and most certainly over alien threats.

In an era of the politics of nostalgia, such an identification acquires political salience in the wake of male fears. Threats foreign and domestic returned men not to nostalgia for the certainties of romantic democracy but rather to the precivilized force of anarchic individualism. Reagan began to be attributed with the charismatic qualities of the Wayne-figure, by contrast to his opponents.

Ronald Reagan was asked after his 1980 debate with Jimmy Carter whether he was scared or nervous on that stage debating the President of the United States. No, he replied, he was not; after all, he had been on the same stage with John Wayne. This remarkable statement conveyed several popular images at once—Carter was not manly, and we need manly values in a President; Reagan was not afraid of the "effeminate" and gentle Carter because he had somehow "stood up to" the supermasculine Wayne; thus Reagan had the same manly qualities as Wayne so sadly lacking in Carter. The fact that Wayne was a symbolic icon created by popular culture and that the President lived in a very real political world did not dissuade Reagan from making the identification. Reagan instinctively understood Wayne's importance to a vision of what America stands for, distinct from the moral and peaceful homely, valiant yeoman of Carter's vision. Carter was a figure mired in the realities of the present who warned of a future of limits and compromises. Reagan was a figure who represented the myths of the past as a guide to an unlimited and uncompromising future that reprises that past. For Carter, history was a tragic reality; for Reagan, history was a romantic fiction, and fiction won the day.

Reagan represented a tradition of white male power that was not shared as ardently and confidently by black, Hispanic and Jewish males, and certainly not by all American women. For this tradition is another way in which white male power tends to the kind of anarchic individualism untempered by woman as civilizing force and threatened to destroy the familial core of the peaceable kingdom by the capacity for violence that male heroism held as necessary. But it was important in both the elections of 1980 and 1984, since the hard core of Reagan's support came from white males. The other side of the "gender gap" was that Reagan was throughout seen as a "man's man," a recrudescent representation of true manhood, while Carter and Mondale were seen in feminine terms as something less than manly. In 1984, Reagan was viewed by many men, Democrats among them, as "two-fisted," "tough" and "macho" as opposed to his opponent. Published reports caught this male voter perception of the romantic virtue Reagan represented: "He's a man who, when he says something, sticks to his guns," said one. "It's a John Wayne type of thing, you know, the Cavalry." "Reagan can butt up against the Russians." To some younger voters in 1984, Reagan "comes off as a father figure" who is strong and forceful. Indeed, in a New York Times/CBS News Poll taken late in the campaign, among the age group 18-to-29, the men preferred Reagan to Mondale by 57 percent to 30 percent, while women preferred Mondale to Reagan by 46 to 41 percent. People describing Reagan used terms like "bravado," "swagger," "swashbuckle," "tough guy" and so forth. Like Carter, by comparison Mondale was described as a "weak male," "perfect gentleman," "courtly manner," "part of the Brie-and-chablis crowd." It appears that people associated Reagan with a masculine ideology and attitude and Carter, Mondale and other Democrats as feminine, weak, and thus ineffectual (Baas).

It was in the atmosphere of the desire for violent decision that Reagan emerged in 1980. He had long advocated violent decision in a wide variety of international conflicts, ranging from Ecuadoran tuna boats to his statement that if he had been President when the hostages were seized, he would have given the Iranians a time limit ultimatum after which Iran would "cease to exist." But more than that, in his popular imagery and rhetoric, for many people Reagan represented Western values brought into the contemporary world. Both his lifestyle and his political advocacy made him seem to be the Wayne-like hero who would serve us well as an outlaw hero-President standing up to our enemies, such as the Iranians holding our women and children hostage. He communicated an image of the "quintessential hero of the West—the town marshal. Accenting this image were his origins, the West (California—the last frontier); his penchant for Western garb, his ranch, his pastime of riding horses and several of his film and television roles; and his physical appearance: tall, lank and rugged. Like the savior for the West, he exuded honesty and sincerity, innocence, optimism, and certainty" (Fisher 302). When he was shot, Reagan displayed the aplomb and fearlessness we associate with the Western hero who carries on despite his wounds. As the Lone President, he could represent a nostalgic tradition of male heroism drawn from the Western myth in the contemporary political world. Reagan's political re-enactment of romantic heroism in the modern world was not looked upon by everyone in America and abroad as a good thing. It seemed indeed that we were going to show the world that our heroic mythology was going to prevail, regardless of the consequences.

The recrudescence of Western heroism in the contemporary world re-emerged with the frustration over the hostages taken in Iran in 1979. With the Iranians spitting hatred at us and chanting "America can do nothing," Americans revived their most archaic mythic story: the captivity narrative. From the accounts of Puritan ministers' wives captured by the Indians down through dime novels and movies, the story of Americans, especially women, held against their will by aliens has been a compelling cultural folktale. Although the story has been retold in a variety of contexts, both real and imagined, we still associate its mythic resolution with Western heroism. One of the most powerful images in the tradition is the rescue by a hero leading the cavalry in to save the beleaguered settlers surrounded or held hostage. Our inability to make the realities of the Iranian crisis live up to the mythic adequacies of the captivity story created an intolerable gap between our expectations for popular narrative and our ability to make manifest those expectations. An expert on terrorism, David Hacker, said shortly after the seizure of the hostages that we want "cinemaphotogenic solutions" in the manner of a John Wayne: "People like this because it is like the movies. If that is inapplicable, we have a sense of national frustration because we can't play Wild West there. Tehran is a big city, close to the U.S.S.R. We can't just jump in and say, 'We'll show those bastards whose mythology should prevail' " (qtd. in Worthington). Carter, of course, did sense something of the lack of mythic resolution to the hostage drama by sending in the cavalry in the form of a rescue mission that failed, serving to increase the sense of national frustration and dooming his chances for re-election.

The stage was thus set for the emergence of a figure associated with the promise of Western mythology. Reagan's self-associations with the promise convinced many that he possessed the charismatic ability to bring about a resolution of the stalemate that lived up to the requirements of the story. He appealed to a nostalgic sense of our own mythic prevalence, that the archetype of the Western hero could still exercise the kind of effective action that would resolve the stalemate by the rescue of the hostages and the punishment of their captors. The release of the hostages just after Reagan was sworn in suggested to those who had invested in his identity with the myth that it was still powerful. But the difficulty remained that the myth was limited by the incongruity of myth and event. Reagan seemed unable to apply the charismatic power of the mythic identity during the TWA hijacking in 1985, with the same attendant public anger and frustration at an inability to bring about mythic resolution as Carter's crisis of 1980. On the other hand, in the Grenada invasion of 1983 he appealed to our fears about the repeat of a captivity narrative and argued that he made the preemptive attack in order to prevent other dark-skinned aliens from holding Americans against their will. Similarly, his confrontations with Khaddafi, limited though they were, evoked memories of the uses of shootouts against evil. But the rhetorical heat was not matched by violent military actions large enough to provide mythic resolution of enduring world conflicts or even local defiance from villains such as Khaddafi, Ortega and myriad Islamic terrorists. Reagan represented the Western myth to the world without undue risk.

But the inappropriateness of the myth to the contemporary conflicts and the unwillingness of many Americans to see it through to a large-scale bloody end did not abrogate the desire to see it represented. The popular roots of the myth were, after all, aesthetic, a creation of popular fiction. So for Reagan the Western myth was in large measure of popular ritual action, actions that represent the myth without unduly endangering it. The ritual involves taking a heroic stance of defiance and vengeance, promising, for instance, "swift and effective retribution" for attacks on American citizens. The ritual calls for a cycle of self-casting as a wronged innocent and alter-casting as the epitome of evil, a ritual release through military theatrics, resulting in inconclusive alteration of forces and intent but allowing us a ritual of resolution, symbolically resolving the unresolvable (Jewett and Lawrence, "American Civil").

Ritual re-enactments of a mythic archetype restrict our expectations of it, but they also belie our doubts about its relevance or effectiveness. Indeed, it can be argued that the myth has been transformed into a degenerate form: since we no longer believe in the myth of effective individual action, we have turned to a more elemental and defensive myth of the violent avenger, who does not create community or enforce justice but rather acts as an agent of asocial revenge. Such an agent defends Rockwell without necessarily believing in it or redeeming it. If that is the case, the Rockwellian moment is past, and The Town is not in a state of creation but rather in a state of decay.

The myth of the violent avenger without clear moral or community purpose other than the representation of revenge has been celebrated in popular tales such as *Death Wish* or *The A-Team*. In the 1980s, perhaps in response to the persistence of frustration and anger (especially among males), the political icon of Johnny Rambo enjoyed considerable popularity. Rambo was a thoughtless, sexless and vengeful killing machine, an image of a muscle-bound superpower whose spirit had been held captive by the betrayals of both our government and our enemies. Once unleashed, he destroys both Vietnamese and Soviet foes with impunity. But his vengeance is beyond good and evil, a national force directed at any hostile target. Reagan himself was touched by the savage directness of the representation, remarking while waiting to go on TV and announce the release of the TWA hostages, "Boy, after seeing *Rambo* last night, I know what to do the next time this happens."

Reagan's own representation of the Western myth was not charismatic but rather elegiac, a ritual re-enactment of a decaying archetype. It seemed to stem from an attitude of romantic pessimism, that the romance of violent individual resolution could no longer be counted on. The celebration of Western heroism as a ritual suggests a kind of popular heroism that fabricates heroism through political play without the powers and resolutions associated with its original form. Indeed, such a degeneration of our most fundamental heroic myth of male power may be part of a more general decay of the belief in progress. Progress in American mythology has long been a function of the myth of effective individual action, and if its Western representation has transformed it into ritual, it has become something that defends but does not create, protects but not progresses, an archetype that has lost its mythic connections with broader moral and social purposes (Cawelti).

If Reagan had represented himself as solely a latter-day model of the Western hero, he could not have become President. Indeed, his Western image as a "hipshooter" with a penchant for violent action created political difficulties for him. But the attempt to portray him as beyond civilization failed, since the central image that was a key to this popularity was as the Stewart-figure. Reagan's Wayne manifestation was muted, even undermined, by the fact that people saw him as a sociable part of The Town, a man who was nice and easy-going and kindly, not capable of blowing the world up in a missile shootout. It was as if that many people did not take the tough talk and militaristic breastbeating too seriously, that his belligerence was an occasional frivolity emerging when we were challenged. Reagan's popular appeal was more broadly based in his inhabitation of, and leadership of, The Town itself. His was not primarily a romantic fiction of war, but rather of peace, the peace that was the mythic promise of the merger of individualism and community. A President cannot be an outlaw, and the Wayne-figure must remain outside the ken of social order, a figure of the romance of violent founding. The Stewart-figure combines the traits of individual self-reliance and community responsibility in a mythic identity that enjoins social leadership and emulation. He is not a charismatic archetype of pagan independence, but rather a charming archetype of social inter-dependence. If he retains lessons from the Wayne-icon, it is that violence defends The Town. The lesson the Stewart-icon teaches is that the myth of effective social action, tempered by the creation of social peace, is possible and even necessary for the continuation of the Rockwellian moment into a progressive future. The Stewart-figure of *Liberty Valance* builds on the original myth of violent founding to lead Town and Nation. His mission as a romantic hero is idealistic: to stabilize and further popular order as exemplified in The Town (Cawelti 192).

Such a figure, a candidate for boy-mayor, is of and in The Town. He is the agent of popular order by being an integral part of it. He is the Guy Next Door, the Nice Guy who finishes first, a trustworthy innocent for whom honesty is the best policy, but who is no Pollyanna and certainly nobody's fool. He is normally a peaceable man, but is no sissy or milquetoast. He is earnest, honest and hardworking, but tolerant of human failings and genuinely altruistic, although he doesn't think anyone should get a free ride. He is ambitious and not against the good life in moderation; but he has known enough of the dark side of human nature to know that excess is as bad as deprivation. He is eternally young, clings to a tenacious optimism and belief in progress and warms to people rather than ideas. He is the pivotal icon of The Town, the archetype who represents the idealized myth of popular order that still has a nostalgic grip on the grassroots mind.

The Stewart-figure, then, serves as a model for male social adjustment and institutional stewardship in The Town. He must find adventure within the confines of domestic institutions; express his individualism as a leader of community; and balance worldly success with the responsibilities of social roles (Sklar, "God and Man"). For the politics of nostalgia, this requires male acceptance of a fundamental task that qualifies him for his community position: his role as head of a family. In Hollywood's most famous rendering of this myth, *It's a Wonderful Life*, Stewart learns of his centrality to the health and happiness of the community. His yearning for adventure, individual freedom and worldly success outside of the community is constantly thwarted. But through the responsibilities and joys of family life, he settles into understanding the value of familial roots and how that serves as the institutional basis for his community leadership. At every crisis, George Bailey (Stewart) is renewed by wife and children, by the adventure of domesticity that enriches and stabilizes his life. His independence to act in the world of business outside the home is motivated by his understanding of the importance of family, his and the other families in the community to whom he has a responsibility. His pursuit of worldly success (unlike that of the Scrooge-figure, Potter, his archrival) is both legitimated and tempered by the fact that he acts for them. He abandons the charisma of precivilized independence for the charming normalcy of domestic happiness. The primary myth he represents is the familial basis of popular order.

Woman as Civilizing Force

The popular order of the Rockwellian moment is rooted in the male hero's acceptance of family as an embrace of community values and responsibilities. But like the founding of The Town itself, the founding of the Family in cultural mythology must be rooted in an emotional bond and not a rational calculation. The initial impulse that civilized the American male was romantic love, or what has been called "the myth of proper sexuality" (Cawelti 184). Not only did romantic love direct the potency of male power away from violence and toward domestic passion, but also it placed sex and sex roles in the context of institutional approval.

It was in the Age of Jackson that a "cult of true womanhood" began to be celebrated as the normal role complement to true manhood. The popular image of the ideal citizen and Presidential candidate dates from then, continuing with remarkable consistency to the present: a man who awaits the verdict of the people by his hearth, surrounded by his faithful wife and adoring children, accepting wholeheartedly the roles of husband, father and homebody. He is civilized by sentiment, tempered by the love, counsel and piety of woman. The familial home is the province of woman, the castle of domestic tranquility. As a man domesticated by romance, the male hero's province of social and political action outside the home is on the side of civilization, since the pursuit of wealth or war serves the higher function of defense of family and the popular order it enjoins. Charity, church and related "good works" were the province of women, but family also gave the male a reason for social heroism that is not anarchic. Potter's asocial greed in *It's a Wonderful Life* is proven to be destructive (through the fantasy of "Pottersville"), while George Bailey's familial sentiments suggest action motivated by social utility.

America has long been represented by two monumental icons: Uncle Sam, a symbol of male power, and the Goddess Liberty, which symbolizes the promise of maternal solicitude and benevolence. The popular icons of American womanhood have traditionally not been quite so Junoesque, but they do offer a promise of benevolent care and domesticized romance rather than orgiastic seduction. The various images of mother and wife—the Girl Next Door, the Wise Mother, Betty Crocker, the Domestic Wife—that have traditionally been associated with the nuclear family are archetypes of female heroism. For the heroic dream of the family is complementary—mutual icons that offer identity with each other, circumscribing a system of support for each other that defines the nuclear unit of The Town. In large measure, this conception of domestic heroines stems from the cult of true womanhood that defined female roles. The romance of womanhood was not heroic eroticism, but rather heroic domesticity. The basic female role in the nostalgic popular order was as civilizing force. Civilization was based on the stabilization of personal life, the "private values" that served as a bedrock for social dependability. The myth of proper sexuality excluded the destabilizing lure of Eve's delights on the one hand and activities outside the home that endangered love, marriage and family and engendered androgynous tendencies. Reagan's mother and wife, at least in their popular images, are offered as iconic representations of female heroism.

Reagan's representation of the traditional family includes both his account of his family as a child and his family life as husband and father. In the former instance, as we have seen, the idyllic boyhood is flawed only by the goodhearted but alcoholic father who was "a sentimental Democrat who believed fervently in the rights of the working man, [but] also believed that every man should stand on his own two feet." But Reagan's mother was the icon of civilizing true womanhood. From his mother, young Ronald Reagan learned the love of drama and the "fundamentalist Christian beliefs that even today strongly mark his letters, his conversations, his speeches and his actions." Consistently Reagan is later pictured in his official propaganda in the spirit of the campaign biography as "the captain of a family": "Home, with his wife and family, is the governor's favorite place. That's where he is happiest and relaxes the best. He adores and admires Nancy, his wife, and is a good friend and father to his children...." Ronald and Nancy Reagan are a "shining exception" to the usual toll taken on political couples. Nancy

never felt neglected, because he never allowed business to push her to the background. At the time, she fully understood her husband's responsibilities and took a great interest in what he was doing. Although she was careful never to interfere with his official duties, she was—and is—not afraid to speak her mind if she felt the staff pushed the governor too hard. The Reagans are totally devoted to each other.

And Reagan wrote this to his son Mike when he was getting married: "There is no greater happiness for a man than approaching a door at the end of the day knowing someone on the other side of that door is waiting for the sound of his footsteps" (van Damm).

Not all official propaganda obviously deals in cultural idealism, but like the other tales of the public Reagans, all this was designed for political image-making. But certainly it placed the Reagans in the tradition of romantic democracy, that for all their success, wealth, power and access to the super-rich, they still retained the simplicity and faith that made their family happy and united, and by extension should serve as an example for the American family. Reagan, however, was the first divorced President and thereby probably did more to legitimate divorce than any other political figure. He seemed strangely distant from his children. Certainly the Reagan children were as diverse and rebellious as most contemporary families. Since they rarely gathered as a family unit, true adherence to tradition seemed strained.

But as with so much else with Reagan, it was what he represented and not what he did in "real life" that was important. Reagan as the "captain of a family" was a symbolic leader whose authority was grounded more in his popular attitude than his personal rule of his family or in his political rule of the American family. Nancy could be admired as representing the concerns and emotions of ordinary women, despite her devotion to conspicuous consumption. For feminists Nancy was the epitome of the aging debutante, the feminine representation of the American Dream as defined by Mattel's popular Barbie doll, a little girl's fantasy of Cinderella and Prince Charming (Ken) as defined by the culture of the 1950s. But with her enactment of female bourgeois theater, Nancy has been very much in the tradition of woman as a civilizing force as amended by the popular culture of the post-World War II era from which she emerged. She was obviously more of a richly-born and -bred glamorous lady than the plain-but-happy wives of 1950s TV situation comedies, but as with her husband it was her popular attitude about women's roles in society that won partial mass appeal. For she seemed able to provide popular mediation of female elegance and simplicity, youthful attractiveness and grandmotherly concern, moving from jetset super-rich parties to sponsoring foster grandparents and drug abuse programs. She belonged to a pre-feminist generation that civilized the home, be it the American Gothic clapboard farmhouse, the 1950s suburban home, or the White House. She presided over state dinners and her husband's favorite macaroni-and-cheese, fretted over the condition of the White House and ghostwrote an article for *Family Weekly* entitled "What Thanksgiving Means to Me." If her husband seemed to exemplify the anarchic individualism and violent potential of American manhood, this was tempered by his public love for Nancy, calling her "Mommy" and deferring to her tastes in their private quarters in the palace they had sought so long. She belonged in the cultural tradition of true womanhood, an apolitical and deferential adjunct to male heroism.

By contrast, Jane Wyman, Reagan's first wife, disappeared from Reagan's official biographical material, since their divorce was an embarrassing episode in the popular epic of his happy, fated and uninterrupted rise to fame, wealth and power. Indeed, their courtship and marriage had been touted by the fan magazines and gossip columnists such as Louella Parsons as proof positive that the American Dream of a stable and happy marriage and family life was possible in the glamorous and hedonistic world of swinging Hollywood. "In America," wrote one observer, "people *believed* in the movies, finding in them not only glamour but moral verities and hope that they sometimes did not find in religion, or politics, or the mundane realities of their lives....At a time of endless Hollywood scandals, they (Ronnie and Janie) were proof that Hollywood had 'just folks,' good people who got married and lived by the moral standards of small-town America. In a country without royalty or aristocracy, Americans wanted their movie stars to inhabit a magical other world and yet to be like themselves" (Leamer 111, 115). They were an ideal couple only in the symbolic reality of popular idealism as communicated through fanzines, and the bubble burst with their divorce. But the image of woman as marital and familial civilizing force survived this setback and was revived and accepted by Reagan's successful popular representation of his happy marriage to Nancy.

The Cinderella dream is important to keep alive, especially when dramatized as a political representation of both glamour and moral verities as the First Family. Ronald and Nancy Reagan successfully mediated themselves as a kind of democratic Prince Charming and Cinderella who did indeed have a happy ending to their story, living in a palace, wearing elegant clothes to lavish balls and riding in sleek and shiny coaches, far from the reach of the common herd but living out both our desire for the validation of moral verities and our yearning for glamour.

We have spoken of the American Adam, our "the plain old Adam, the simple genuine self against the whole world," in Emerson's phrase. But is there an American Eve? The traditional myth of woman as a civilizing force portrays true womanhood as exemplified by a happy, busy and useful First Lady, in the context— and confines—of marriage and the family, and who is content with that. Such a symbolic ideal is likely to be devoid of the cunning, aggression and libidinal energy and freedom associated with the

Eve figure. Freed of their role as a civilizing force, women could become aggressive: so from this viewpoint, "women's liberation" produces devouring women with masculine traits whose secret motive is to emasculate and dominate men. Thus sexual and economic freedom for women is both a psychic and social threat to social order and leads to the mythic and political celebration of American woman in her traditional image. It may even be the case that such traditional roles are celebrated the most ardently at precisely the historical moment they are becoming inadequate, more complicated, or irrelevant to the way we live now.

The Other Side of Town

The cultural myths on which The Town is founded are ideals, and thus can be denied or changed. But it is in the nature of myth that it is evoked as coextensive with the world, since "antiworlds" or "subworlds" which are not part of it constitute parts of Town beyond the reach of consciousness. Myth involves both reaffirmation and denial, since those outside the mythic consensus embody the possibility of contradiction and subversion. If it was the case that the Reagan representation involved the myth of the universality of the nuclear family as the core of community, then its reaffirmation was crucial. "Despite the pressures of our modern world," Reagan said in his 1986 State of the Union address, "family and community remain the moral core of our society, guardians of our values and hopes for the future. Family and community are the co-stars of this great American comeback. They are why we say tonight: Private values must be at the heart of public policies." But it was the Family of The Town that comprised this image, and in such Magic Kingdoms there is no evil, or more commonly, evil lurks in the failed families beyond the pale on the other side of Town.

This is the Gothic underside of the myth, the repressed consciousness of a dark side to the Rockwellian moment. Michael Rogin has pointed out how much *King's Row* is an American Gothic nightmare, with evil lurking not only across the tracks in shanties and whorehouses but also behind the lace curtains of respectability: the bourgeois family is beset by dark relationships and secrets, such as incest, sadism, domination and violence: "The protection men need in *King's Row* is not the protection of family but protection from women" (Rogin 57). Similarly, *It's a Wonderful Life* offers a frightening glimpse of what Bedford Falls could become without the grace of familial connubiality by being transformed into the dark Gothic Nighttown of Pottersville. Denied access to proper sexuality, women there have become either prostitutes or spinsters and the community has deteriorated into savagery—bars, pawn shops, bistros and brothels, cynicism, exploitation and meanness. Both films show possible consequences of the absence of woman as civilizing force and what America kept fearing from the 1940s on—that it was becoming a Town without the mythic underpinnings to resist the decline of tradition and more specifically the rise of the new woman. Without women acting as civilizing force in the community, the moral relativism and sexual freedom so feared by Reagan and other conservatives of his generation undoes the basis of The Town.

Thus in the politics of nostalgia, the desire to restore traditional female heroism was not wholly a reassertion of patriarchy based on a fear of female equality. But it was in a cultural sense a desire to see women "put in their proper place" again. That proper place in the iconography of The Town is not only within unambiguous sex roles, but also in the role of moral civilizer. Reagan instinctively sensed this in his famous offhand remark to a Republican women's audience about how men would still be in "skin suits" and "carrying clubs" if it weren't for women. But even if women sensed condescension toward the "gentler sex" by Reagan and his all-male cronies, the historical tide of women's entry into education, the job market, access to mobility and even power, suggested even to them that there was no going back to true womanhood. Perhaps they shared the fear of evangelical ministers who saw in the changes of women's position in society the decline of American civilization, but Republican support among upper-middle class and urban women and other realistic appraisals obviated any draconian attempt to restore a role structure that was largely mythical to begin with and historically defunct in postmodernity.

Even if there was a strain of romantic pessimism about the decay of true womanhood and therefore the fate of civilization, this did not stop the widespread desire to see the nostalgic model of The Family celebrated, and those that represent its negation denigrated. Such symbolic politics occur in the wake of a politico-cultural lag, wherein cultural mythology, supported by generations of popular images, is threatened by social change that undermines the promise of adherence to the myth. Since the myth retains enough popular salience to require political mediation, Reagan's task was largely a symbolic one.

What was required was symbolic celebration of woman as a civilizing force and symbolic annihilation of women who threatened to "decivilize" society. Symbolic annihilation involves rhetorical and political condemnation, trivialization and exclusion of those women who represent a threat to the nostalgic model. The threat of sexual freedom—unrestrained eroticism, abortion-on-demand, birth control, open marriages, easy divorce, enjoyment of pornography, sexual experimentation and so on—can then be symbolically attacked by equating their advent with the feminist movement and other "liberal" trends. Symbolic celebration, on the other hand, extols the virtues of the traditional family, while at the same time paying obeisance to the many accomplishments of women outside the home. While claims for "comparable worth" and "equal rights" are annihilated, the hope is also held out for female progress if action is confined to a proper role structure and cultural mythology is believed. No better example of this process existed than the "Dear Mr. President" special broadcast by NBC-TV on June 5, 1983. In the story, a little girl decides that she will be the first woman President some day and writes Reagan asking to visit, since she wants to get a head start on "getting the hang of it." After several plot twists, she is indeed asked into the heady confines of the Oval Office, where Reagan himself tells her "to stick to your dream" and maybe someday it will come true. Through symbolic celebration, her claim to be a Presidential candidate is legitimated, but only far into the future, changing nothing about female access to power in the 1980s. So through celebrating a future Horatio Alger claim that offers hopeful fantasies, the male gender maintains its control over social and political power.

The relegation of "bad girls" to the Other Part of Town was a political act of symbolic denial, a denial of female archetypes that suggest forms of sensuality or sensibility that date beyond the 1950s. For the politico-cultural lag impels seeking and finding a nostalgic locus in popular culture. The logic of nostalgia is to find in the past the answer to the present, symbolically denying the present in favor of a past with a sure iconic structure imagined in popular artifacts. The 1950s offered the 1980s, or at least Reagan's following, the latest possible historical purification setting, the last imaginable mythic time in which the Family was at the institutional center of local self-government. The "purified" woman of such a setting is devoid of the taint of post modernity, mediating for a later time the model of an ideal female Self. The threat constituted by The Other Woman is absent from that past, denying the legitimacy of their existence. Even though they exist in the present, they constitute a threat to legitimate female identity and thus must be denied here too.

The Reagans represented themselves as part of that amended form of romantic democracy, the bourgeois normalcy of the 1950s. In lieu of the impossibility of annihilation of the present, they offered themselves as a First Family who symbolically celebrated the popular image of that time. The Reagans were a 1950s family, representing for us not only nostalgia for the stable suburban family of *The Donna Reed Show* or *The Adventures of Ozzie and Harriet*, but also the abandonment of the guilts and fears of the Gothic underside of Rockwell. The re-formed family of the 1950s accepted affluence and moderated glamour as the reward for adherence to the nuclear model. They could boast of their origins in the mythic place of Rockwell, but also legitimately enjoy the fruits of their labors and confidently lecture the children on the role requirements of the American Dream. Reagan represented himself as the principal cultural authority who, as father of the First Family, knew best. He did not accept as legitimate American history since the 1950s, substituting instead the pseudohistory of our popular mediated experience. His authority was that of Robert Young and Ozzie Nelson, as the civilized paternal head of the American bourgeois family. But to represent the authority of that nostalgic vision, Reagan could not show any knowledge of the nightmare vision of George Bailey's odyssey through the Other Side of Town, nor display doubts and fears about the Gothic underside of respectability in *King's Row*. His was the authority of the autocrat of the breakfast table, presiding over the suburban Utopia of affluent normalcy. His authority was that of the patriarchy of benevolent fathers that had dominated domestic television of the "placid decade," at the same time Rockwell's celebrations of familial power and rectitude dominated the covers of *The Saturday Evening Post*. He was the product of our idealized conception of what a father, or even a grandfather, is supposed to be, as mediated by a wiser and older Ward and June Cleaver presiding over a sanitary and complete bourgeois universe devoid of deprivation or rebellion (Schickel,

Intimate Strangers 194-200). Reagan's admirers in the 1980s responded to such magical incantations as a way of redeeming history since the 1950s, attempting to "re-open" history and give it a new and happier ending, only if we had listened to his wisdom and not been lured by the folly of the Other Side of Town. Prospective atavism not only makes a claim on the future by applying old values that will "shape our dreams" there, but also a claim on the past, practicing selective amnesia about history since the fall of Rockwell. It was as if the 1960s and 1970s, the civil rights movement, Vietnam and Watergate, the sexual revolution and the legitimation of fun in the Other Part of Town had not, or perhaps should not, have happened.

As moral representations of the community, then, Mr. and Mrs. America stood as a bulwark against the encroachments and temptations of The Others who would subvert The Town. Their stance was a symbolic posture, conveying their opposition to history and the shared belief that the restored American family will live happily ever after. They were extraordinary representations of the ordinary, enacting popular proof of the historical determination of the reformed American Dream and moral loyalty to the memory and illusion of the glory days of normalcy. Familial authority in the American Town implied a commitment to place, to the perfection of community as identified by the proper role division between man and woman. The posture might have been "dated," as Geraldine Ferraro charged, without much actual correspondence to personal or social reality. But in the politics of nostalgia, it had much salience. So the public posture of the Reagans involved self-depiction as the paradigm devoted bourgeois couple. An NBC "news special" in 1985 solemnly photographed the First Couple on their "favorite date" at Camp David, watching a movie, eating popcorn and holding hands. Such orchestrated glimpses of the Reagans helped defeat the charge that they comprised a regal presidency with opulent tastes and super-rich friends, far from the model of bourgeois normalcy they affected. "Queen Nancy" became in 1981-82 so much the symbol of uncaring aloofness that a cautious, organized White House effort was mounted to reform her image, largely by associating her with the civilizing functions of true womanhood and showing her with a taste for the casual and ordinary. This included highly visible Christmas-time visits to a Washington children's hospital, visits to schools to speak against drug abuse and to hug children, and even hints that she was the power behind the throne, urging her husband to make peace with the Russians. The politics of symbolic posturing involved orchestrated photo-opportunities as outward and visible signs of personal concern, even though critics felt it was a deception. Senator Weicker, for instance, in 1985 indignantly pointed out to Congress that a White House celebration of handicapped children presided over by the First Lady was being held at the same time the Reagan Administration was cutting funds for handicapped children. Yet it was the symbolic gesture on the part of Nancy Reagan that was important, since she represented the personal concern of true womanhood, who did not want to seem heartless. It is true that such posturing is a pseudo-action, but it was characteristic of the Age of the Reagans: the picture was the story, and policy actions such as cutting funds were relatively unimportant.

Mrs. Reagan's reformed role involved her in the symbolic dispensation of good. The posture of benevolent caring was central to the image of the true woman, the bastion of private and legitimate charity and social education. She was also the epitome of the fulfillment inherent in the monogamous marriage, given the moral imperative of acceptance of the reformed-1950s role structure. She was an icon of femininity, devoid of the devouring or aggressive traits so fearful in "liberated" and "political" women since. Implicitly, she stood against the threats to middle-class normalcy, in particular the threat of unrestrained eroticism and the passing of the 1950s-model nuclear family.

American history since World War II was witness to rapid changes in female role expectations and choices and created an identity crisis for women. Both men and women came to fear the implications of a new female identity—erotic liberation, the rejection of marriage and parenthood, the claim to equality and access to formerly all male roles, even the value of androgyny. Nancy Reagan was a symbolic icon who served to protect the myth of the female ideal of true womanhood in its revised form. As a community leader, she celebrated the role structure that restricted "what women are supposed to do." As a homemaker, she celebrated the "I'm a lucky girl" role of maternal "caretaker" of husband and children. In both cases, she was supposed to be instrumental in the production of "good children": a partially civilized and obedient husband and children who would perpetuate traditional notions of distinctive male and female heroism. (It was, of course, unimportant that in fact the Reagan children were not "good children" in this sense, insisting on living their own lives in the changing American milieu—talented Ron, Jr. becoming a contributing editor of *Playboy* magazine and spunky Patti Davis being named one of *Ms.* magazine's 1985 women of the year and writing a semi-autobiographical novel about growing up in a governor's mansion and having to deal with a detached father and cold mother.) For that historical moment, however, Nancy Reagan celebrated the popular order that denied the prospect of the triumph of the Other Side of Town, especially the sexual freedom it implied.

The complement to that role was that her husband, as "First Man," stood in erect posture as the symbolic defense against evil, and as such had to protect the sanctity of the popular order by the denial and punishment, through violence if necessary, of those from the Other Side of Town (and the Other in general) if and when they constituted a threat. Even though the commitment to institution and community meant male acceptance of society, the "social contract" between the individual hero and the popular order included the proviso of defensive violence. In Reagan's time, this included attacks on The Other in the form of identifiable and "defeatable" targets, such as Grenadan Marxists and Libya's Colonel Khaddafi. But male dominion in defense of The Town also includes defense against domestic enemies. Reagan postured himself at various times as the defensive representation against Hollywood Communists, Democratic cryptosocialists, Berkeley radicals and welfare cheats, appeasers and "give-awayers," big spenders and unilateral disarmers. The American male hero is both social paragon and extralegal killer, capable of loving his own children and bombing the children of the Other.

Like other fictional American heroes before him, Reagan was able to concentrate in one identity belief in the constraints of society and the dream of legitimate vigilante force, the innocent strength of the social hero. This allowed the symbolic expression of "true manhood" in an age when its dominance and independence was threatened, both by defeat in war and by the threat of feminism. How much latent male fear of "devouring women," "castration anxiety" and social emasculation and androgyny Reagan mobilized is impossible to say, but it cannot be discounted, given the persistence of a "gender gap," an "aggression gap," between men and women, and the undeniable fact that in the Reagan Era, men associated "effeminate" characteristics—compassion, fairness, negotiation, nurturing, gentleness, reconciliation and the like—as evidence of "softness" (Baas 10-11). (In a new way, feminists were often in the position of the classical true woman, trying to civilize amoral male aggression both outside and inside the home.) Reagan's assault on "women's issues," such as day care, abortion, welfare, school lunches and comparable worth, can be seen as punishment of women associated with the "promiscuity" and "unrespectability" of the Other Side of Town. As the symbolic defense against evil, the male hero was compelled to be punitive not only toward aliens abroad who would threaten the popular order, but also aliens at home who are not part of the family of belief.

The Family of Belief

The Reagans, then, represented themselves as cultural icons of heroic American experience. Icons are models of sacred importance, objects of veneration and ornamentation that give shape to mythemes as they are adapted in different ages and for different purposes. In the 1980s, anxieties about the persistence of the institution of marriage and the role structure surrounding it apparently gave rise to the need for familial icons that reassured us of cultural continuity. The Reagans were idols of the tribe, much of whose political strength lay in their ability to represent a mythical family of belief. The family of belief are the "good people" of The Town, those whose loyalty to the promise of belief and rejection of rebellion, skepticism and disloyalty gives them dominion over the moral and material prosperity of the American Village. Ronald Reagan's policy making may have belonged to Wall Street and Nancy's Hollywood regality to Rodeo Drive, but as iconic performers of the American family melodrama they belonged to Main Street. Their unabashed babbitry struck a responsive chord in the domain of Our Town, among those who craved the normalcy that Hollywood and TV had so long celebrated and that now seemed incredibly to be slipping away. But it is often the case that the more comprehensive or quick historical change is, the more adamantly that people wish to deny that it is happening at all. The Reagans could do little about the vastness of historical change, but they could invoke "the Canute principle": they could not command the tides of history to cease, but they could assume an iconic posture in commanding them and thus attract mass admiration and veneration. But the relentless sweep of the tides went on anyway.

The politics of nostalgia in the 1980s occurred in a climate of opinion that included not only a wistful celebration of popular pseudohistory but also a diminishment of the family of belief that might have given such a celebration of restorative powers. Despite the Reagans' laudable performances in domestic bourgeois theater, the family after The Fall increasingly varied from the 1950s model. Nostalgic representation, it seems fair to say, had its limits. The Reagans ruled a mythic domain that offered the analogical truth of the popular past as an infallible guide, even if there was little expectation that the country would somehow return to an imagined familial normalcy. Nostalgia here appealed not only to the warm simplicity of a "primal scene" of fable, but to our fear of the unknown chasm of the future. It was as if we had peered into the abyss and found it wanting: lacking confidence in the Dream of popular order in the future, we invented a dream-state of innocent familial command, a mythography that locates truth as a province of the past. Thus Ronald Reagan ruled an imaginary state with dominion over the family of belief.

It was often said that Reagan governed in poetry rather than prose. The prosaic stuff of budgets and arms control was not his strong suit. Rather it was his poetic ability to evoke, both in mythic word and iconic self, the domain of the past. His rule was a popular sovereignty over a kingdom of shadows, allowing neglect of the present and disregard of the future. Reagan was not so much an ideologue espousing a forensic ideology as he was an idealogue representing cultural ideals. The imaginary state was a mythographic country where ideals have been perfected, wherein there is nothing to fix and time has stood still. It was a state of artful innocence, in which we could sleep in the dream of popular order and familial authority.

Yet such insubstantial re-imaginings of the imaginary state were in large measure a theatrical exercise in political elegiacs. There was a kind of playful discontinuity to it all, as if people found in the First Family a satisfying popular ritualization of domestic bourgeois theater in poetry, without having to fear draconian efforts to re-enforce a familial model in political prose of policy and law. They were the innocent ambassadors from a timeless kingdom, armed with the self-righteousness of the representation of cultural authority. They enacted the elegy of political consolation in dramas of national sorrow, self-congratulation and wrath. They were the mourning "national handholders," symbols of reassurance during events of national trauma, such as the Challenger disaster. They led the garish extravaganza of the rhetorical reassertion at the rededication of the Statue of Liberty in 1986. And Reagan himself was the vessel of wrath by visiting popular vengeance on Khaddafi, the symbol of antiworld hatred of America. As heads of the family of belief, they expressed the much-desired illusion of parental omniscience, the elegiac ideals of our imaginary state.

The Reagans were romantic icons of a partial community who shared a unified suspension of disbelief. They had all consented to believe in the iconic powers represented on the political stage. The Reagans vouched for the efficiency of ritual through ritualized sorrow, ritualized benevolence and ritualized aggression. They dramatized the equation of the political and the familial and became the ornaments of an age that shared little continuity with the past save through their reassurance that the observations of familial ritual insures the success of popular order, at least in the timeless world from which they came. Their authority was beyond dispute because it was not of this world. It was a serene dominion, full of the adoration of political romance and devoid of the fallibility that one experiences with actual and varied families coping with the imperfect knowledge and discontinuity of contemporary history.

Chapter Three
The Business

In the nostalgic model of the Rockwellian American community, the core institution is the business. Sentimentalists might argue that the rock of the American community was the stable nuclear family, the devout might claim that it was the church and high school principals that it was the school, but the more hard-headed have always known that the central institution of American society was, and is, business. We have always been more of a Hamiltonian than a Jeffersonian society, a commercial order that knows the value of a buck. Americans have always appreciated the importance of money, the rewards of work and the social utility of greed. The popular consciousness of the grassroots mind was long ago convinced of the benevolence of local business, and the businessman was integrated into the community as a respectable citizen on whose prosperity the other institutions of the Town depend. In his civilized role, the American Adam is a cultural hero who creates prosperity through the exercise of his Puritan virtues of industry, sobriety, thrift, frugality, punctuality and so on. The American Dream of success and material reward is open for all in the Land of Opportunity. The hero's quest in business is a legitimate one, an example of the essential harmony of private motives and the public weal.

Orators of the time saw Andrew Jackson as a representative symbol of business success through the development of his character, assuring his rise to prosperity and power. "The character of the American people," noted one, has been the sole cause of their growth and prosperity," noting that the Puritan founding fathers built no almhouses because they tolerated no paupers. Concludes Ward, "One who tolerates no paupers can justify his lack of charity only on the grounds that paupers deserve their poverty. This is the obverse of the belief that man succeeds because of himself; he also fails because of himself." Ward points out that early American efforts

71

to help the poor included exhortations to adopt the inner virtues that had served successful men like Jackson so well in their climb to prosperity and power and that American society was a "fair field" in which the competition for economic opportunity guaranteed just outcomes for rich and poor. An inauspicious beginning was an impetus to escape the rigors of poverty and seek success. As Ward points out, "Although wealth and powerful connections might sometimes, even in republics, bring success, they more often brought the impotence of indolence; poverty is the breeding ground of success" (Ward, *Andrew Jackson* 213). Here is one of the primal American attitudes, the essential justice of the unequal distribution of wealth and power, that whatever lot people have in life they almost always deserve; that wealth is a sign of God's favor for one's hard work and frugal habits and that poverty is a sign of God's disfavor for sloth and sin. "Mind your business," Benjamim Franklin had early on warned; those who did mind their business were rewarded and those who did not were not.

These popular equations about the way the world works have had a powerful grip on the grassroots mind ever since. The local self-government of romantic democracy is dominated by local small businessmen who represent business values as a dynamic force in the harmonious operation of the institutions of the Town. The myth of capitalist benevolence is supported by the Church and the School, and the businessman reciprocates with his support of the functions of the other institutions. The businessman moves easily in a moral universe untroubled by the ethic of acquisitiveness and the necessity of high consumption and debt on the part of buyers; if corners have to be cut and deals sharp, this demonstrates good business acumen and not moral turpitude. There is no equation between material and moral bankruptcy, but on the contrary there is an equation between moral and material prosperity. The moral contract of the community allows the businessman leeway in the conduct of business in return for his support for the institutional order and his money-back guarantee of material prosperity.

There are potentially antisocial and amoral tendencies in the ethos of capitalism, something that runs against the grain of the settled life of the American peaceable kingdom. The mythological unity of American life could be unsettled by the unleavened ethic of unlimited acquisition and exploitation, in which the capitalist is there to ravage and not serve the prosperity of the Town. Like the fly-by-night banks and snake oil salesmen of Jacksonian America, the businessman then becomes a demonic figure of fraud and flight, a con artist like the railroad lawyer of American legend who tried to fleece the good people of the Town out of their life savings and farms. Further, the businessman in this image lives up to his popular reputation as a stone-hearted skinflint who transforms all the world and heaven above into one gigantic ledger into which every human relationship becomes a cash transaction, eliminating human sympathy and Christian love from the world (Scrooge, Silas Marner, Uriah Heep, Mr. Potter). The danger of anarchic individualism derived from the mad pursuit of more and more wealth at the expense of the community was understood by Melville in his demonic figure of Captain Ahab who brought ruin to his world by his hateful pursuit of Moby-Dick:

Only one was saved, one who came to the recognition that the world was a joint-stock enterprise and that in love, not pride, lay human salvation. Ahab had turned his back on home, wife, and child; Ahab was the man of will who excluded all human sympathy from his heart. The whole drama of Moby-Dick is an enactment of Ahab's defiance of the power that rules the universe. Melville's most terrifying insight is the suggestion that at the center of the universe there is nothing: that blind chance, not God, rules; that there is no meaning. (Ward, *Andrew Jackson* 111, 113)

The captains of capitalist enterprise would rule a truly social Darwinist world of prideful acquisition based on an inhuman ethic of the survival of the fittest. But a society of Ahabs would be an anarchic struggle of fierce, driven, competitive individuals worse than even Karl Marx could have imagined.

The problem for the American popular order was and is how to make the cultural world safe from the potentially unbridled egoism of the businessman by incorporating the legitimate role of businessman into the American imperial self. The businessman in this popular image was accorded a legitimate, indeed primary, place in the community if he accepted the restraints on egoism and pride that the strict economic logic of capitalism seemed to dictate. The institutional contract of the Town involved a culturologic which modified the savage antisocial tendencies of the capitalist; if Ahab had to be transformed into a hypocritical but thoroughly tamed Babbitt, then so be it.

Having made the capitalist entrepreneur over into a model citizen, American political culture could then devote itself to extolling the virtues of the classical businessman of Rockwell even when he and the virtues he embodied have become more and more historically obsolescent. Wrote Geoffrey Gorer:

The ideal situation is envisaged as a man alone with his raw materials, using his industry, ingenuity, and know-how to make two blades of wheat grow where one grew before, to produce better mousetraps in ever-increasing quantity until they are available to everyone who has a mouse. This is the vision. This is the picture which accounts for the quasi-religious overtone given to the phrase "private enterprise...." In the imagined golden age of equal independent producers no other relationship than that of the willing buyer and willing seller was necessary as envisaged; but such a simplification, if it ever existed, has not existed for a long time; and so there is posed the great problem: What is the role of other men in the world of things? (Gorer 153, 161)

The benevolent model of classical capitalism has long been an essential part of our popular folklore, and orators have long pointed with pride to the material prosperity of the country as a product of the spirit of enterprise. The nostalgic myth includes a world of small businessmen and tradesmen and shopkeepers who provide the goods and services necessary for the "joint stock" contract of benevolent capitalism. For in the grassroots mind lingers the myth of the small business entrepreneur who runs his business on a human scale and contributes to the peace and prosperity of local self-government. Americans still like to remember themselves as essentially a nation of shopkeepers, small businessmen who retain their commitment to the peaceable kingdom.

The function of this attitude served to give the businessman a legitimate place in the community and remind him of his social responsibility to the folk culture of local self-government. But what is astonishing is its persistence into the contemporary age of gigantic international corporations and banks remote from Main Street. The American corporate super-rich still sincerely express their belief in their own altruistic contribution to the good of the community, and corporate propaganda still persists in expressing their belief in local self-government and benevolent capitalism. In 1984, *Context*, a publication of the DuPont Corporation, ran an issue entitled "America's Communities," which began:

Today community initiatives are partnerships on the rise. Such evolution is not new but now it is driven by necessity. Funds are tight and federal priorities have been redefined. Most important there is a rekindled desire for self-sufficiency. Communities work better when they work together, when local citizens determine their needs, marshal their resources and shape their responses. This issue examines the resiliency of local institutions, the resourcefulness of citizens and the renewal of communities across America.

One article featured a color picture of Reagan speaking at a black elementary school in Washington, the article arguing that business and other "local" institutions are solving problems at the local level without reliance on Big Government (*Context*). It also reveals a sincere belief in the benevolence and harmony of American institutions and their essentially local nature. The myths of romantic democracy persist in the boardrooms of the Fortune 500, providing recrudescent justification for corporate activity, even though they are far from the world of the village shopkeeper. The Ford Motor Company is a multinational corporation, but its founder built Greenfield Village as a celebration of romantic democracy, representing the story of how capitalist tinkerers—Ford, Edison, the Wrights—transformed and enriched life in America, although ironically creating the industrial conditions for the demise of small independent business and the eclipse of much of the power of local self-government. In historical sites such as Greenfield Village, the mythic power of the past is invoked, re-minding us of our nostalgic roots and infusing Reagan's power to represent the myth of capitalist benevolence into the present.

The Age of Reform

Reagan was born in the period historians call "The Progressive Era," precisely the first period after the close of the frontier and the industrial and urban revolutions that transformed the country relatively quickly. This was one of those historical periods in which many people's lives do not conform with their beliefs, so political reforms served the purpose of attempting to reshape life and thought. The Progressive period:

"...was a rather widespread and remarkably good-natured effort of the greater part of society to achieve some not very clearly defined self-reformation. Its general theme was the effort to restore a type of economic individualism and political democracy that was widely believed to have existed earlier in America and to have been destroyed by the great corporations and the corrupt political machine; and with that restoration to bring back a kind of morality and civic purity that was also believed to have been lost." (Hofstadter, *The Age* 5)

The Progressive reformers juxtaposed "the agrarian myth" with the new urban and commercial realities of the time: "The more commercial this society became...the more reason it found to cling in imagination to the non-commercial agrarian values....[T]he agrarian myth came to be believed more widely and tenaciously as it became more fictional" (Hofstadter, *The Age* 24, 30). For the Progressives, the agrarian myth was a nostalgic cultural referent, and the rhetoric of Progressivism had a strong reactionary sentiment. Reform would revivify the grassroots democracy of small enterprise and commerce that had been lost in the onrush of urbanization and industrial conglomeration. As Woodrow Wilson put it, progressive reform was "for the purpose of recovering what seems to have been lost...our old variety and freedom and individual energy of development."

A political order that equates reform with recapturing an idealized past means that politics is always backing into change, believing that we can control the future by making it into the past. The American Dream is a nostalgic dream, but not simply the worship of a lost world; rather it is the recurrent belief that the American Dream can actually be recaptured. When Reagan said that "our best days are ahead of us," he meant that the economic future would be bright because our renewed spirit of enterprise and adventure would be imported and updated from the past. Americans truly do not anticipate the future, but rather anticipate the past in the future. This seems to stem from a keen sense of insecurity after the great economic difficulties beginning with the Great Depression; the American "usable past" is used to reassure us of the mythologies of our origins and their applicability of "first principles" in the future.

It is in that sense that Ronald Reagan was an economic reformer, as spokesman for those economic first principles that were practiced in the Town. In that sense, he was a progressive reactionary, reassuring us of the mythic validity of that nostalgic economic past of his Illinois-heartland origins. Indeed, not only was he accorded representative status as the spokesman for an old and renewed democratic capitalism, but was also a complementary spokesman for the primacy and superiority of business over government. In that sense, Reagan was a popular authority who spoke for business and also a popular counter-authority who spoke against government, thus helping to delegitimate government's claim to be the primary institution of the society. Reagan reasserted the primacy and benevolence of business by invoking not only the folklore of capitalism, but also the folklore of government (Hofstadter, *The American* xxiv, xxxv).

In the former instance, Reagan celebrated the legitimacy and efficiency of private enterprise and in the latter instance denigrated the illegitimacy and inefficiency of public enterprise. Reagan could thereby portray himself as a progressive who wanted to bring business efficiency and a good "business climate" to government, but also as a reactionary who wanted to "get the government off our backs and out of our pockets" and believed government to be hostile to business. The many anecdotes he told over the years about business success and government failures may have been largely fictional folklore, but they served the purpose of illustrating that both business and government were going the wrong way: business acceding to government regulation and "creeping socialism" and government doing heavy-handed and unproductive things to stifle business.

Whether all this was true was subject to considerable skepticism, but it made Reagan into both a reactionary and a reformer, in which the mythic business past would become the reformed future with a more passive and helpful government. Indeed, the popular appeal of "supply-side economics" was in its nostalgic simplicity: like the Town of yore, all indigenous institutions, government included, depend upon the prosperity of business; if government is a hindrance to business activity and profits, its own tax base suffers, as then does the Town; if it helps business, then profits bring in more taxes with which to finance better schools, private charity, religion and so on in an upward spiral of local programs. So too with the popular culturologic of a "balanced budget": in the nostalgic model of local self-government, all the institutions of the Town adhered to the simple rule that "you can't live beyond your means," so too should government. Similarly, the disharmony of business and government is overcome by returning and restricting government to what Reagan always rather murkily called "the legitimate functions of government," which in its more extreme social Darwinist manifestation was restrictive indeed, eliminating welfare, agricultural and regulatory functions. With Reagan, the popular myths of "the law of supply and demand" and "unlimited growth" were returned to what business believed to be their rightful place in the American pantheon of economic folklore.

The folklore of capitalism views government as a necessary evil, a potential Leviathan that by its very nature can violate the contract of romantic democracy and unduly impinge upon the rights and privileges of the other institutions of the Town. For in the grassroots mind is the recrudescent attitude that government grows at the expense of other institutions and indeed becomes an agent of evil. Americans have long been accused of holding to the paradoxical attitudes of "pro-democracy" and "anti-government," and nothing could express this better than the notion that the very government people believe to be the product of God's blessing and *vox populi*—the institutional expression of democratic choice—also turns out to be a notorious wastrel and irresponsible meddler in people's private business. Some of this is blamed on "bureaucracy," which the grassroots mind associates with both Big Government and Big Business, both of which are bad influences on the peace and prosperity of local self-government. But big business is still business and can be made competitive by that most American of devices to maintain the myth of capitalist free enterprise: anti-trust laws. Government, on the other hand, can become confiscatory and oppressive, indeed an alien Other who interferes with the legitimate life of the Town.

The primacy of business values in their popular folklore about government can be seen in two distinctive attitudes, cost-cutting and poverty. Business believes that government can only be reformed from its spendthrift ways by imposing business values and "sound management" on government and curbing what Reagan recurrently called government's "tax and tax, spend and spend" habits, reinforcing the popular view that "you can't solve problems by throwing money at them." Reagan appointed a commission of businessmen, headed by business tycoon J. Peter Grace, to study ways to control costs in government. Grace was of course appalled and recommended $424.4 billion in spending cuts and great reforms to make the government bureaucracy "efficient" like business bureaucracies. That many of these cuts were politically unlikely only served to reinforce the business view of government, i.e., if government were run more like a business and less like a "bureaucracy," taxpayers would save billions of dollars. In any case, discovery of government waste justified their contempt for the ability of the government to accomplish anything, and by logical extension, justified their belief that governmental "social engineering" is not only illegitimate but doomed to failure by the "bureaucratic" boondoggling of its programs. Cost-cutting not only becomes a tragic necessity but also a moral imperative that restores government to its limited "legitimate functions."

The same popular business attitude defined the Reaganesque image of poverty, its causes and cures. As we have seen, charity has not been a universally held American-capitalist value, and certainly not charity administered through taxation and the redistribution of wealth. Charity in this popular image is the province of females, taking pies to old widows and food baskets to the shanty on the edge of town on Christmas Eve. Charity then is private and voluntary, administered at the grassroots level; if it is public and involuntary, it is inefficient, confiscatory and bad for both rich and poor, since it punishes the prosperous by taking their money and giving it to the supposedly indolent who use the help to support their idleness, giving them no incentive to work and become self-reliant. In his more extreme manifestations before becoming President, Reagan was fond of characterizing Social Security as "welfare" and the graduated income tax as "Marxist." But in more general terms he represented the business view that public charity was bad because it was bad for business and labor.

Reagan represented the folklore of government to the business class that supported him. His speeches over the years usually included anecdotal horror stories about the mismanagement of poverty programs, evoked images of great hordes and droves of welfare cheaters living in luxury and cast doubt as to whether those who were poor deserved help or indeed wanted to escape their condition. This included explanations of poverty that argued that the homeless were "homeless by choice," that people go to soup kitchens to eat because it's free and convenient, that food stamp recipients can buy vodka with stamps, that poverty doesn't destroy character, rather people with no character prefer to stay in poverty. "It's not so much," wrote one observer, "that the poor deserve to be poor. It's that they *choose* to be poor....It's as if life were a voting booth and those at the bottom were freely pulling a lever marked 'misery'." The mythic assumptions to explain poverty, then, center on a business view of motivation, which bristles at the thought of being exploited at the expense of the shiftless on the take. Reagan said in 1980:

Food stamps have become a massive subsidy for some of the exotic experiments in group living you have read about. Many taxpayers find it difficult to understand why a seemingly able-bodied and otherwise self-supporting individual can walk up to the grocery counter with a basketful of T-bone steaks and lay out free food stamps, while they are buying hamburger with hard-earned cash.

From the point of view of the grassroots business mind, this is an inverted moral universe and indeed a universe that only could be rectified by the elimination of support for sloth. Further, individual and community prosperity, both material and moral, would be enhanced by taking away benefits and instilling the initiative to work and achieve out of poverty (Easterbrook 18-19).

For his followers, Reagan righted the moral universe and reasserted the legitimate cultural heroism of business activity and the right to the material and moral rewards of heroic economic achievement. Reagan not only represented business values in government, he also represented, by example, appointment, association and praise, the essential heroism of the business person as the exemplary social actor of the country. His appointments to high office were very largely successful captains of industry, and his Cabinet was a a virtual "board of directors" of America, Inc. His friends and political associates were largely the super-rich of southern California, and he often spent holidays ensconced in the *latifundia* of the overlords of Palm Springs. The ranch, the millionaire status, the living well made Reagan a Presidential representative of individual economic opportunity and the legitimacy of opulence. Not only did this relegitimate the heroism of business acquisition, it also justified business dominance of government, since successful men from the business world would bring the right values and approach to the conduct of government. This was a variation of the business politics of the Reagan period— the myth that professional politicians who never met a payroll got us into this fiscal and welfare state mess, so it will take "non-political" professional businessmen to get us out.

Reagan and his business-oriented administration, then, would re-form government to support private economic heroism. But here is an American dilemma that is insoluble because of the incompatibility of values that Reagan, and other metapolitical figures before him, have tried to represent and resolve. The extreme social Darwinist strain in the grassroots business mind seems too harsh, but any toning down makes economic heroism seem less than heroic, introducing elements of guilt and doubt into the social role of the businessman. The "rugged individualist" businessman becomes a popular symbol of the American Dream of freedom and opportunity and reward for heroic virtue, the entrepreneurial adventurer whose risk-taking made America great and strong. But in its unsullied form, the businessman escapes any social responsibility; indeed individual freedom becomes incompatible with social responsibility and thereby a threat to the community. But since confiscation and control of wealth is illegitimate, it becomes difficult to condemn bigness, although bigness violates the nostalgic image of the independent small entrepreneur competing in an open market ruled by supply and demand. Further, bigness becomes difficult to control, dominating markets, resisting responsibility and making the business corporation into a vast bureaucracy that courts the danger of becoming remote and inefficient. Indeed, Reagan represented the myth of benevolent small-town capitalism while surrounded by people drawn from big business. Business domination of government in the Reagan era was rooted in the grassroots folklore of capitalist benevolence and the folklore about government that justified business values in government.

The Reagan business coalition saw government as a *service industry*, an industry whose main "legitimate function" was to serve business. If business was the primary institution that served the Town, government was a secondary institution that was supposed to serve the operation of capitalism and thereby produce material prosperity. As Gorer wrote:

To improve the design and increase the supply side of things adapted to man's use and enjoyment is the most important object of life. This object is pursued with a fervor and a sense of dedication which in other societies and at other times have been devoted to the search for holiness and wisdom, or for warfare. Any device or regulation which interferes, or can be conceived as interfering, with this supply of more and better things is resisted with unreasoning horror, as the religious resist blasphemy, or the warlike pacifism. It is against such a background that the interpretations given by most Americans to the abstractions Freedom and Opportunity can be understood. Besides the right to do what one likes, when one likes, without the interference of authority, Freedom means, over and above everything else, Freedom to make more and better things, without external interferences from government or sentimental do-gooders. (153, 161)

Prosperity "trickles down" through business prosperity enhanced by the "good business climate" characteristic of the institutional harmony of romantic democracy updated into the era of the global reach of multinational corporations and banks.

This popular image of the centrality and supremacy of business in the idealized American community goes a long way in explaining Reagan's, and by extension many of his supporters', attitude about a wide variety of things. If the government is the institutional industry that serves business, then it follows that its "legitimate function" is to create the attitudinal climate and material conditions for business prosperity. Not only does this obviously mean a tax structure that rewards success, the control of inflation rather than unemployment, spending shifted to the defense industry from support of the underclass, it also helps explain Reagan's lukewarm support of environmentalism. The "machine in the garden" is not there to preserve nature but rather to exploit it. The activities of Secretary of the Interior James Watt became symbolic of this attitude: public lands are to be used for mining, timber, gas and oil and other economic purposes rather than enjoyed for their aesthetic values. From the point of view of environmental groups such as the Wilderness Society and the Sierra Club, Reagan's environmental policies were a betrayal of the public trust by giving private interests access to the wealth of public lands. Environmentalists advanced the notion that somehow the wealth of those lands, as well as their beauty, belong to "us" as a people and should be preserved for posterity. But from the point of view of a business philosophy that observes no "public interest" beyond the sum of all private interests, resources that are not being exploited now are being wasted in the sense that profits can be made from them. The business logic of it was clear enough to them, and they thought the "environmental lobby" sentimental do-gooders who had silly notions about reclaiming strip-mined land, saving endangered species and opposing clear-cutting trees.

Some of this attitude stems from the myth of unlimited resources drawn from the past, but even those that recognize the limitations on resources still may support their exploitation now, because of the business logic of present accumulation without "planning," the freedom and opportunity to utilize resources and the limited perspective on future consequences. Economics takes precedence over aesthetics: when Reagan supported the private cutting of the redwood trees in California, he remarked, "A tree's a tree—how many more do you need to look at?" A 1984 Sierra Club magazine article sensed the same attitude: Reagan, the article argued, saw America in nostalgic terms wherein the freedom and opportunity of each self-interested individual exploiting his environment was socially compatible, a world in which all people pursued their own interests, with little concern for risks, the impact of economic activity on one's neighbors, or the needs of the future. Reagan's environmental policy rejected the concept of present responsibility for stewardship of the environment for the future, scoffed at concern over environmental risks as "softness" and denied a sense of community, seeing America instead as an exploitative "one-generation society" (Pope). Perhaps that is overstated, but the point here is that limited perspective on consequences is characteristic of the grassroots business mind, which exalts the primacy of utilization over the claims of the natural order. Nor is this attitude anything new, since the history of America includes the wholesale destruction and consumption of much of its natural resources, which from the point of view of grassroots business logic was crucial and necessary for the creation of American prosperity.

Perhaps this helps explain Reagan's 1976 representation of the popular attitude at the grassroots level that opposed the Panama Canal treaty, which proposed to eventually relinquish American control of the Canal. Reagan, running the Republican primaries against Ford, sensed that the issue of the treaty hit a popular nerve, and he used it to his advantage. The popular nerve was a complex and irrational one, stemming from the sense of American retreat in the world, giving in to the dictates of a small country and failing to exert power to maintain the outposts of the American empire. But the way Reagan phrased his objections took it into the business realm: the treaty was a "giveaway," almost as if it were a gigantic international version of food stamps: "we bought it, built it, paid for it, maintain it, and should keep it." Reagan seemed to be saying that the Panama Canal was a great national example of government-business cooperation, wherein government as a service industry built the canal to serve national business interests by facilitating commerce, bringing in revenue in tolls and of course maintaining strategic hegemony over the region to let trade follow the flag. Among other things, giving up the Canal was bad business, relinquishing national property that had been bought and paid for. For Reagan, then, this was simply another example of how wrongheaded and badly managed government was, since it did not seem to know the value of, or our "sovereignty" over, such a valuable national property, nor that government's primary role was to defend property, private or public, to support the common wealth (Reagan, "Introduction").

Finally, Reagan represented the recrudescence of the grassroots business attitude toward labor. In the classical nostalgic model, labor does not constitute an organized union and certainly not a subordinate class; rather the ideal labor force is a collection of self-regarding individuals who freely sell their labor in the marketplace, like the businessman who hires and fires them, and who value their freedom and opportunity for economic mobility above economic security and union solidarity. As rational actors in the free marketplace, their motivation to work is sound, their mobility unlimited and their pride in a job well done for a fair wage a pillar of economic morality. Those who are unproductive or unemployed owe their failure to individual and not systemic faults, such as laziness and drunkenness. This belief in a classless society and the essential harmony of business and labor has persisted despite the concentration of business power, unionization, structural unemployment and the imbalance between labor skills and what the post-industrial employers require. Reagan represented this view during the height of the 1982 recession in which he observed that he read employment ads in the papers and found plenty of jobs that would go wanting because no one will take them. In other words, like in the small-town shop or factory of yore, all labor need to do is apply and work. There is here, of course, no sense of Marxist exploitation, nor any milder notion of conflict or business responsibility to the community; there is rather Reagan's appeal to "simple solutions," harking people back to the nostalgic harmony of business and labor, boss and worker, effort and reward. The proper division of labor in society is based on the imagined social roles of benevolent capitalism and a responsible work force.

In the nostalgic model we remember an organic community in which institutions help and support each other. The free market works with the *help* of government, so there is no "separation of business and state." Government declares and advances business sovereignty, the primacy of business values and interests, the cultural heroism of economic achievement and sees itself as an institutional force that serves the community by serving business. If this interpretation is correct, then Reagan's admiration for and identification with Calvin Coolidge should not surprise us. Coolidge was a nostalgic figure even in the 1920s, when he took pains to be photographed haying (in celluloid collar and patent leather shoes) to establish his agrarian roots, much as Reagan was photographed cutting brush at his ranch. Coolidge extolled the work ethic in others, but like Reagan hardly kept a Spartan schedule as President. He associated with and admired captains of industry who, like Reagan, he saw as the true heroes of American business culture. As Governor of Massachusetts, Coolidge suppressed the Boston police strike of 1919, declaring that there never was a right to strike against the public safety; similarly, Reagan decertified the air traffic controllers in 1981 with the same argument. Coolidge also sent Marines to dabble in the internal affairs of Nicaragua.

But perhaps at a more mythic level, from the perspective of the 1980s, Coolidge is the very image of the frugal town mayor who presided over the prosperity of the American community. Coolidge provided mythic mediation of business sovereignty during the 1920s, running the great boom economy of the time on the values of a small town (one can imagine him the mayor of Grover's Corner, New Hampshire). Coolidge's grasp of the complexities of international economics and his commitment to the economic absolutes of the grassroots mind were illustrated by his attitude toward the repayment of war debts by bankrupt and starving European allies in World War I: "They hired the money, didn't they? Well, let them pay it." Reagan was a less Scroogean figure than Coolidge, but no less representative of the tradition of business sovereignty over government.

Indeed, despite the innovations of the New Deal and Great Society, despite breathtaking military budgets and an unimaginable national debt, the economic continuities between the Coolidge and

Reagan presidencies were striking. Coolidge, like his political descendant Reagan, saw the prosperity of the 1920s as a product of the people's capitalist heroism. "The main source," he declared in his last State of the Union address in December, 1928, "of these unexampled blessings lies in the integrity and character of the American people." Part of the reasons for those blessings was Coolidge's optimistic trust and support of business sovereignty and his acquiescence in business control of government. The 1920s were a "good time" for a great many people, particularly because business and government, as represented by Coolidge, said so. Coolidge was a popular figure who presided over economic growth, but it only benefited part of the population—the richest part. Farmers, the poor, blacks, southern whites, ethnic slum dwellers and others didn't share in the boom and were to suffer greatly when the boom turned to bust in the 1930s. But even during the Coolidge era, "Fine old-English houses with high gables, leaded glass, and well-simulated half-timbering were rising in the country club district, while farther in town one encountered the most noisome slums outside the Orient" (Galbraith 7). Indeed, the achievement ethos of 1920s had reached such levels that everyone seemed to be playing the stock market, investing on margin and expecting the boom to go on forever; it was a fantasy land in which people desperately sought wealth and opulence, "an inordinate desire to get rich quickly with a minimum of physical effort," supported by the "mood of the Twenties and the conviction that God intended the middle class to be rich" (Galbraith 8, 11).

One could see this in the Reagan years. Real economic growth under Reagan was not as great as it seemed, and there were troublesome signs that the prosperity was more a myth than a reality. While there was opulence and conspicuous consumption at the top, there was desperation and hopelessness in an increasingly large bottom of society. But like the Coolidge era, the capitalist ethos of the time permitted no discouraging look at the "other America" who didn't share in the new wealth, nor consideration of where the renewed business sovereignty over government would lead us. Like the Coolidge Era, the "Reagan prosperity" was as much the product of mythic politics which gave new impetus to the myth of American economic destiny, the will to believe that riches can be made quickly and easily by achievers without negative consequences and that the opulent good life was the legitimate individual right of the haves with no social responsibility nor concern for the have-nots. Reagan represented this "new spirit" of an "Opportunity Society" in which "you ain't seen nothin' yet" (quoting Al Jolson from *The Jazz Singer* of 1928), since "our best years were ahead of us." One can almost see the ghost of Coolidge speaking through him, the same economic mythology and trust in business sovereignty that characterized the 1920s, while ignoring the stubborn fact that it was the excessive greed of those American people of "integrity and character" and the sovereignty of business over government that discredited the frugal town mayor and his successor Hoover. "A rising tide lifts all boats," Reagan was fond of quoting; but after 1929, a precipitous sinking tide lowered all boats onto the economic shoals.

Reagan presided over an economic recovery that was at least in part rooted in popular credulity, a will to believe in the continuity of the heroic quest for individual economic wealth and the myths of capitalist benevolence and business sovereignty. "All people," wrote Walter Bagehot, "are most credulous when they are most happy" (Galbraith 28). Reagan could not have become a representative popular figure presiding over a metapolitical age in which nostalgic economic mythology was reasserted and government re-formed accordingly unless people wanted to believe. "No one can doubt," predicted Galbraith of the "lessons" that could be learned from the crash of 1929, "that the American people remain susceptible to the speculative mood—to the conviction that enterprise can be attended by unlimited rewards in which they, individually, were meant to share" (194). It was, and is, a matter of faith in the promise of American bourgeois virtue and its rewards. But the credulous are always ready to believe on slight or uncertain evidence, and their undue readiness to believe makes them ignore or condemn those of little faith. Thus Reagan's representation of that faith was believed despite the jeremiads of economic naysayers and soothsayers alike.

Reagan offered general hope for the national economic future, reaffirmed people's wavering will to believe in their own economic future, and relegitimated the social utility of greed as an expression of individual achievement. Reagan re-activated and mobilized a recrudescent and salient popular attitude toward business success. During the Reagan period, argued political scientist Leonard Freedman, "there have been a steady increase in the values of personal success as against wanting to contribute to social causes.... Reagan's devotion to the entrepreneurial spirit fits neatly with the attitude shift among young voters. Reagan doesn't tell people we are in an era of limits. He says the Republican Party is the party of opportunity, and young people are responding to that." Since the early 1970s, in surveys of college freshmen, those calling "philosophy of life" an important goal declined steadily, while by the fall of 1984 those that listed as their top value "being very well off financially" had gone to 70 percent, a landslide (qtd. in "University Students").

This identification of the young—and for that matter, the older "Yuppies" (Young Urban Professionals)—with Reagan was so extensive that, ironically, the much-discussed "generation gap" of the 1960s ("You can't trust anyone over thirty") now was reversed: veterans of the 1960s didn't trust their own conservative and self-regarding children and bitterly denounced their alleged lack of altruism, compassion and intellectual interest. Critics condemned the young of the 1980s as unabashedly greedy and self-indulgent future Yuppies with no sense of economic injustice or social consciousness. The triumph of Reaganism among college students prompted the old 1970s radical Abbie Hoffman to reverse the dictum:

I don't trust anyone under thirty, frankly. I just don't trust young people. I feel sorry for them because they have given up a part of their youth. There's no exploration or romantic impulses. They're really just young adults trying to impress older adults.... Campuses today are about as exciting as watching TV bowling. (qtd. in Timms 4)

The students of the Reagan era did attach themselves to a romantic impulse, the recrudescent business heroism of romantic democracy that Reagan represented for them in an era in which doubts about their own personal and financial success were overcome by reassurance. Popular credulity is an act of faith, a faith that the individual believes was justified if borne out by events. Those who cast their first or second vote for Reagan on the hope drawn from his unbounded confidence in the legitimacy and probability of personal economic success based on heroic achievement would live to see if that faith was borne out in their own lives.

Back to Basics

"In Ronald Reagan's vision of the future," said Walter Mondale during the campaign of 1984, "the American Dream of opportunity for all is replaced by the ethic of survival of the fittest." But as we have seen, the popular tension between equality and achievement has never been finally resolved. For each new era in American history, the fundamental conflict of these values in the American identity breaks out again. If the generation of students and Yuppies of the 1980s defined themselves as heroic new achievers, it demonstrated the recrudescence of what we may call the "Old Deal," the persistence of values through the politics of the New Deal of the 1930s and its successors in the Fair Deal and Great Society. The Old Deal persists in the grassroots mind and in the contractual and institutional arrangement of local self-government. The Old Deal is the nostalgic model of economic fundamentalism in the popular mind, a fundamentalism based on the simple notions of personal charity and the power of personal motivation. Reagan's power to re-form the New Deal was based in part by his re-presentation of these fundamental notions to older generations who in their popular heart of hearts wanted to believe them, and to a younger generation that wanted an authority figure to expound them anew. We may recall that the economic fundamentals of the grassroots mind were called into question with the collapse of capitalism in 1929. The symbolic political figure who represented the "soundness" of the Old Deal was President Hoover. As Hofstadter wrote:

The things Hoover stood for—efficiency, enterprise, opportunity, individualism, substantial laissez-faire, personal success, material wealth—were all in the dominant American tradition. The ideas he represented—ideas that to so many people made him seem hateful or ridiculous after 1929—were precisely the same ideas that in the remoter past of the nineteenth century and the more immediate past of the New Era had had an almost irresistible lure for the majority of Americans....It is a significant fact that in the crisis of the thirties the man who represented these conceptions found himself unable even to communicate himself and what he stood for. (*The American* 372-73)

It was a significant fact in the 1980s that the man who represented the conceptions of the Old Deal *did* communicate himself and what he stood for and found a popular audience willing to believe again in the economic fundamentals of the past. Reformers were incredulous, but the great majority of middle Americans seemed willing to reinvest their economic identity in the faith of the Old

Deal. The restitution of the folklore of capitalism made the New Deal seem fragile indeed, a blip in the historical continuity of a commercial civilization struggling to regain its confidence in its own economic mythology. It is true that the worsening of economic conditions turns people toward Presidential and Congressional figures that represent change, but "unless reinforced by other factors, does not affect the deeper waters" (qtd. in Goldman 224). Reagan represented those deeper waters and the extent to which the economic fundamentalism is extant in the popular mind. He showed us once again how much we want to believe that the American moral and material system is fundamentally sound.

One major strain in our popular culture has always celebrated the fundamentally sound thinking of "the people" who overcome adversity through their commitment to the Old Deal. It is significant, for example, that during the most protracted crisis of economic fundamentalism, the Great Depression that spawned the "temporary" programs of the New Deal, much popular culture celebrated the canons of the Old Deal. A study of radio comedy during the Depression found that comedy routines helped to relieve the social tensions of the age by "a reaffirmation of traditional American values, particularly the work ethic, success, morality and the importance of the family." Will Rogers in particular represented himself as "a personification of the rags to riches myth." Because of his humble beginnings and enormous success, "he represented the poor country boy who had become a famous entertainer. . . . Despite his wealth and fame Rogers retained his image as a modest friendly cowboy whom money had not spoiled. As a folk and success hero, Rogers reminded Americans of rural values and that social mobility was still possible during the Depression" (Wertheim 510). In a study of Rogers' movies in the 1930s Peter C. Rollins concluded that his:

nostalgic rural dramas document the spirit of the 1930s. . .[T]he late films of Will Rogers portray an alternative society in which the best traditional elements of the American national character have free play. Will Rogers was important to Americans in the 1920s and 1930s because he addressed his humor to their basic sense of rootlessness and loss. . .[H]e somehow bridged the gap between the old and the new.

Rogers' films depicted him as the wise and benevolent senior citizen of "Homeville," who is its, superintending consciousness. Uncle Will has a special insight into the human heart. Because of this special power, and because every problem in Homeville has a human face, Uncle Will is a master of the world. The best metaphor for the perspective given the viewer of the late Rogers films is probably that of a telescope which we look through backwards. The result is that everything appears smaller and therefore less challenging.

If Reagan sounded startlingly like Rogers, that is no accident in the politics of nostalgia.

Reagan, like Rogers, "presented [us] with an image of what Americans had been told to believe was the best in their national character." Following two decades of bad tidings, Reagan supplied reassurances in the spirit of Rogers: "...Americans were indeed fortunate to have such a public person to keep a hopeful image of American values and optimism bright" (Rollins 92).

"Grass-roots America," wrote Furay, "had good reason to mourn" when Rogers died, for he "was its legitimate spokesman, a man who reflected its mind as faithfully as anyone ever has" (2). Reagan, like Rogers before him, could associate with the super-rich but not be seen as a snob. But Reagan could combine Rogers with Coolidge. He could state the case for benevolent cupidity without sounding crass, cast businesspersons as heroes without making them seem greedy, make selfishness seem a moral imperative, and indeed the source of altruism, and portray himself as an exemplar of economic plain truths and simple solutions. He represented in an age of economic peril the myth that the economic fundamentalism of Homeville can be reproduced in the present and future, producing again the personal and social wealth that proves the soundness of the American system and the continued realization for generations to come of the American Dream.

In that sense, Reagan was a popular authority of cultural and economic fundamentalism. The Old Deal for which he spoke was valued all the more as historical change made it remote and nothing of ideological or mythic power appeared on the horizon to replace it. New economic ideas smacked to many Americans as alien, socialistic, or in any case something remote from grass-roots conceptions and personal ambitions. Even though domestic business sovereignty had been challenged by the growth of government, international corporations and banks, foreign competitors and the bureaucratization of the world, the inhuman face of power that history augured could only be countered by an authority that reminded us of the human face of our mythic roots.

As the avuncular host of America, Inc., Reagan did indeed somehow mediate the gap between the old and the new, from the pre-industrial nostalgic small business of the Town to the post-industrial Silicon Valleys of the future, maintaining that the same economic fundamentals apply to both worlds, since in some mythic sense they are the same world in the ongoing American capitalist drama. With his gift of politico-cultural magic, Reagan could see the power of those economic fundamentals when the American economic character believes and practices them, and use our mythic economic past to magically create our bright economic future. Reagan's role as the "superintending consciousness" of American capitalism made him for a time "master of the world," or at least of the world of those who willed to believe once again in the destiny of American material prosperity. There was at this late date in our national (and economic) history a sense of desperation in the reassertion of past economic fundamentals as the key to our individual and collective future prosperity, a desperation borne of a desire to believe despite all the negative evidence to the contrary. With the New Deal receding in our memory, and no coherent alternative ideology in the offing, we could only deal with history by aligning ourselves with a counter-authority figure who represented our telescopic cultural memory of economic prosperity based in mythic history. "Bereft of a coherent and plausible body of belief," wrote Hofstadter, "Americans have become more receptive than ever to dynamic personal leadership as a substitute" (*The American* xxxvi). Reagan represented personal leadership as a substitute for alternative ideas, offering himself as living proof of the fundamental soundness of the Dream. Reagan belonged to an organization called The Horatio Alger Association of Distinguished Americans, which gave annual awards to people who rose above adversity to stand out as role models and heroes.

Hollywood and the Leisure Class

An outside observer might think there is an incongruity in the representation of small business values and archaic capitalist imagery in the present. Isn't it the case that the "Protestant ethic" that undergirds capitalist motivation and bourgeois life is a profoundly stern and demanding moral code that condemns frivolity, folly, fun, spending money for silly and corrupting pleasures, opulence and self-love expressed in expensive things? Is not consumption a temptation to wretched excess and carnal pursuits, and is not leisure an excuse for idle hands to become the devil's workshop? Are not the worlds of the "jet-set" super-rich and the glamorous of industries such as the movies, fashion, music and so forth beyond the pale of the grassroots moral universe?

The outsider observing America is quite right: there is an incongruity here, part of our paradoxical culture. Robert Sklar has put it well:

Americans have always been of mixed minds about great wealth. They agreed it was a desirable goal, but feared the temptations that came with the power of money—the release it gave from ordinary social restraints. They had traditionally been able to condone the accumulation of money more easily than the enjoyment of it.... The situation of the movie stars was doubly disturbing, for as far as the public was concerned the players had just as much fun making money as they did spending it. (*Movie-Made* 77)

The Puritan strain in American culture survives in the economic dictum that it's all right to make and keep a lot of money as long as you don't enjoy it.

Yet the emergence of a visible political and cultural elite devoted to opulent consumption had the effect of reinforcing, rather than undermining, popular belief in the American economic system. For the appearance of a leisure class enjoying the fruits of their success in gaining power, wealth and fame proved the viability of the success ethic. Success in America was never to simply accumulate wealth, rather it was to use money for the freedom it gave you:

Greedy men have often sacrificed virtue and justice on the altar of Mammon, and valued lucre above learning, or religion, or love of country. It is a mistake, however, to deduce the motives of an entire people from the careers of a few representatives, for though some Americans look upon wealth as an end in itself, and sacrifice everything to its acquisition, many more view it only as an instrumentality. The view of the majority squares with that central precept of the folklore of success which says that money has no value except in relation to its uses. (Wyllie)

But what are the legitimate uses of money? People at the grassroots were interested in the leisure activities of the new visible elites: if money gave you any freedom at all, did it not allow you the freedom to have *fun*? Perhaps in Rockwellville there were, for both moral and material reasons, limits to pursuit of pleasure, but could one only envy the rich and mighty enjoying their success through travel, parties, mansions, debuts, balls, yachts, the whole gamut of the "show of society"? Either for purposes of passive vicarious experience, or to find elite figures to actively emulate, ordinary people followed the leisure habits of the rich and famous for their own uses. The "opportunity society" included the legitimate right to use money to have fun, and people at the grassroots sought cues from visible elites on how to consume leisure.

This is the popular function of a leisure class, providing dramatic example through the leisure activities of visible elites of the legitimate use of money for the consumption of fun, and by fiat then extending the opportunity for non-elites to participate in perhaps not as opulent but just as rewarding pastimes as just reward for one's success. A motorboat is not a yacht but it is a symbol of one's success and the right to enjoy consumption as a legitimate expression of that. Veblen wrote,

The institution of a leisure class has an effect not only upon social structure but also upon the individual character of the members of society. So soon as a given proclivity or a given point of view has won acceptance as an authoritative standard or norm of life it will react upon the character of the members of the society which has accepted it as a norm. (166)

Veblen saw ordinary people using a leisure class for "pecuniary emulation," since the elite show them norms of "conspicuous consumption" that dramatize the right to the consumption of fun. Opulence is not threatening but rather beckoning, a lure not only for the pursuit of success in terms of money, but also the legitimation of doing something pleasurable with it. The rise of a leisure class in America corresponds with the historical shifts in this century that brought the wide-spread creation of personal wealth in the middle class, the change from rural to urban and suburban living and the diversification of the American economy including the creation of objects of mass leisure. It is no accident that modern advertising became important first in the 1920s, when the change is most pronounced; the "captains of consciousness" had to induce new habits of buying on installments, desiring leisure objects, devoting less time to work and more to play (Ewen).

It is also no accident that Hollywood as an institution became an important part of this historical process. Both the depictions in the movies and the way the movie stars lived legitimated the utilization of wealth for pleasurable consumption without moral guilt, what has been called "fun morality" (Wolfenstein). Lary May has detailed the extent to which the first two generations of American movies were a learning experience for people trying to cope with the change from a Victorian to a modern world, from a production to consumption economy, from the grassroots community of mythic memory to the new realities of a commercial and urbanized society. The "democratization of consumption" offered the siren's song of mass opulence, the "vision of affluence": "Although the workplace remained regimented and hierarchical and wealth remained unequally distributed, the trappings of luxury had come within the reach of the average consumer." The new culture required expanded "visions of success" that were consistent with the new economic order. Thus the movies became a major way for people to play with new self-conceptions as modern cultural consumers. Mass culture, and movies in particular, says May,

were key elements in the transition from nineteenth-century values of strict behavior toward greater moral experimentation. As the economy consolidated, the leisure arena preserved a sense of freedom and mobility. Both on the screen and in the theater, moviegoers tasted the life of the rich as it was brought within the reach of the masses, breaking down the class divisions of the past. Here was a revitalized frontier of freedom, where Americans might sanction formerly forbidden pleasures through democratized consumption.

Indeed, the themes of the movies and the example of the movie stars communicated to the new bourgeoisie that they could have it both ways, retaining some aspects of traditional morality (marriage) while enjoying aspects of the new material culture (opulence). The movies helped people to mediate the changes, legitimating the new moral order (L. May xiii).

Now it is no secret that entertainment plays an important part in providing role models and social cues for people to emulate, including pecuniary emulation and conspicuous consumption. The cultural paradox is that the stimulation of desires through popular culture gives both credence to, and illusion to, the nostalgic model of proper moral and material behavior. Americans in this century have recurrently felt the "tug" both ways, in recognition and celebration of the superiority of the nostalgic Town, and the lure of consumption which takes then further from the values of Homeville. The paradox remains one of the cultural contradictions of capitalism, and how to deal with it requires popular and political mediation. The movies pioneered the representation of film idols functioning as "national models as leisure experts" who could mediate the tension over changes in values. The stars became "the nation's new aristocracy" who could be

universally loved because they were not socially powerful: they were purely a status group. Unlike politicians or manufacturers, they did not hold authority over large groups of employees or constituents...the force of the stars as popular idols lay in their leisure, rather than work lives. Much of their mystique was that they presumably rose from meager beginnings to become models of success....Power would have been antithetical to their image as playful, friendly people.

Hollywood, both on the screen and in the movie magazines, would serve as a model for the new consumption culture while retaining something of the old—the achievement ethic, the sanctity of marriage, simple virtues as the path to opulence and the way to be uncorrupted by their enjoyment, the balance of work and play, respect for the nostalgic past and the contemporary social hierarchy (L. May 197).

Thus Hollywood, and later on the wider celebrity structure of America, came to serve an important function as a leisure class that was the visible elite that made consumption and the enjoyment of luxury legitimate as a democratic, and not plutocratic, lifestyle. Further, the elite helped to mediate the changes in modern life that tended to undermine the inherited values of the grassroots past. This is no more evident than in the persistence of the myth of romantic love as an emotional touchstone that is both part of the traditions of romantic democracy and a model of conspicuous consumption in the modern present.

Romantic love, as celebrated in popular culture, is a profoundly nostalgic complex of feelings, since it evokes in the present a time-honored tradition from the past: that boys and girls "fall in love" like generations before them, institutionalize those romantic feelings in marriage and the family and live happily ever after, thus expressing the "rightness" and "giveness" of the inherited institutional order. But it also expresses a modern pattern of consumption, a legitimate way for romantic feelings to be expressed in buying. To buy is to be perceived, for the modern consumer culture has defined that one's self is expressed and vindicated in things. The "marriage industry" alone is a vast engine of social consumption centering on that single ritual of the wedding, with diamonds, china and silver, gowns and rentals, catering, gifts, receptions, honeymoon spas and so on. Pecuniary emulation and conspicuous consumption is thus linked to the mythic institutional roots of romantic democracy. "Romanticization of conventional experience," wrote Furay, "is nothing more than a grass-root's fondness for imaginal flights combined with an extension of basic optimism" (57). A social ritual such as the wedding provides a setting for a compromise in the mediation of modern life, celebrating both our continuity with the traditional past in the institutionalization of romantic feeling and our commitment to contemporary consumption patterns.

Hollywood, then, played a mediative role in this process through the romanticization of conventional experience. Both in films and in their public lives, the stars dramatized our popular rationalization of a historical conttflict, overcoming the tension of tradition and modernity that underlay the advent of the consumption economy. But as Daniel Bell and others have shown, the cultural contradiction that the advanced capitalist economy has created has only imperfectly been overcome and no amount of popular mediation can produce totally the credulity necessary to reconcile the tension. The American imperial self, broad as its shoulders are, has difficulty incorporating what may be ultimately irreconcilable values and lifestyles. The classic American Self is the self of the "accumulation culture," the Victorian model of Horatio Alger achievement, in which the business culture hero achieves through legitimate accumulation, producing the social good of capital formation, savings and investment. But the modern addition to cultural Selfhood is the heroism of the "consumption culture," the heroic quest of psychic rewards through leisure activity, which undercuts savings and investment and encourages spending and debt, "living beyond your means." Goaded by advertising, intrigued by changes in fad and fashion, lured by the hedonistic promise of flaunted pleasures, the consumption culture produced by a Self that spurns productivity and overtime, practices patently un-Victorian lifestyles, and finds its self-worth not in work but in play. Pecuniary emulation finds its idols not in the heroes of the accumulation of culture, such as a corporate executive, but in the consumption culture of such symbolic places as Hollywood and Broadway.

The visible activities of an elite leisure class at the top of society can be a source of stability, but also of instability. In the later case, those in the workforce who toil without leisure rewards come to fear and envy the "idle rich." But in America, such a Marxist outcome has not occurred; rather the latter-day leisure class has come to be the *pecuniary idols* of the masses. A famous study of profiles in popular magazines noted the change in this century from admiring portraits of "idols of production" (businessmen, inventors, government officials) in the earlier years to an emphasis on sketches of "idols of consumption" (movie stars, sports heroes and other celebrities) (Dallek; Lowenthal 100-16). Idols of consumption provided us cues for the economic exercise of our new identity. If we could not identify with an idle and stuffy economic plutocracy that had been the earlier leisure class, we could very much identify with a new and more accessible *aristocracy of celebrities.* Observers of American social cohesion have often been puzzled by the extent of the stable social hierarchy and cohesion despite great inequalities of wealth, opportunity and circumstance. The modern American society was not and is not, then, a class struggle, but rather an emulation struggle in which the middle and lower classes desired to be like the aristocracy of celebrities. If the modern definition of self-identity was expressed in a glut of commodity fetishism, it was at least a democratic one, in which the celebrity leisure class functioned to provide vicarious cues for consumption patterns.

The leisure class that emerged first in Hollywood and then expanded into the visible aristocracy of celebrities served a function for business and commerce by becoming pecuniary idols. But they did something else, too. They served the function of popular idolatry, as visible symbols of the consistency of traditional values and modern life, of the non-contradictory nature of production values and consumption values, how consumption is a vital and not decadent force and the legitimacy of conspicuous leisure (Gitlin).

Popular culture functions to mediate past and present, convincing us over and over again that there is no contradiction in the way we lived and the way live and in the way we should live and in the way we actually do live. Popularly mediated nostalgia serves an ideological purpose of incorporating the past into the present and reframing our picture of the past to include the present. At the base of social power is the ability to define reality, and much of popular culture can be analyzed for that purpose. In particular, a leisure class becomes a palpable symbol of the social legitimacy of newly practiced values and consumption patterns, serving the larger ideological function of style leadership. The hegemony of the consumer economy was insured by the leadership of a popular leisure class rather than an elite one. "Hollywood," wrote Lary May, "showed how this scarcity psychology could be overcome, and consumption become a positive force. Rather than luxury eroding the achievement drive, or a society based on open opportunity, it flowed into rising expectations. For as success took on new rewards, as the stars became consumption idols, excess production had a purpose" (197-98).

Over the decades since the advent of Hollywood, the aristocracy of wealth and the aristocracy of fame have become more and more intertwined, until now they are often difficult to distinguish. But the popular aristocracy of fame still functions to mediate popular leisure behavior in now multi-faceted ways. Ronald Reagan became for the 1980s a popular and political representation of the contradictions and incongruities of the American identity as it struggled to balance off the competing claims of work and play, achievement and leisure, production and consumption. He was reassuring to some and irritating to others in his ability to live easily and comfortably with contradictions that other Americans found morally or intellectually incompatible.

Reagan spanned both the Victorian and modern ages and preached both production and consumption values without fear of contradiction. As Dalleck pointed out, "...his identity was also shaped by a post-industrial society where leisure and play held more appeal than work and where conformity and personal charm were more likely paths to success than personal initiative" (8). He was, in an ironic and paradoxical sense, both an idol of consumption and an idol of production. In the former case, he achieved fame and then power on the strength of his celebrity and mediated histrionic skills, but in the latter case he extolled the virtues and legitimate ascendancy of captains of industry and commerce. But it is likely that he will be remembered by both ally and critic alike for his representation of the promise of good and high life as reward for achievement. He represented the merger and ascendancy of a rich leisure class, often "new money," that had no qualms about flaunting it in the ostentatious display of wealth and opulence.

The Reagans were icons of the leisure class, leaders of an unabashedly glamorous and almost defiant leisure class that combined more than ever before the values and lifestyles of Wall Street and Hollywood. Reagan led his ruling class as the head of a new aristocracy of celebrities that gave self-confidence to the rich in their public display of consumption values. Reagan brought to the Presidency a representative figure who incorporated the consistency of traditional values and modern life, making the nostalgic values of business production relevant and compatible with the values of conspicuous consumption of celebrity elites. Reagan gave legitimacy to the pleasurable self, the public enjoyment of riches as a just reward for heroic economic achievement. He brought the relaxed moral climate of Hollywood's pleasure-domes to the more intense corridors of economic power without seeming to advocate decadence and immorality. He represented the self-affirmation that many among the new rich so desperately needed, helping them to overcome any guilt feelings they might entertain about display and overconsumption. At least for the time being, Reagan was the popular representation of not only the legitimate centrality of business activity in America, but also the romantic legitimator of leisure as reward for effort within the loose framework of traditional bourgeois values and lifestyle combined with the freedom and mobility that always had been the promise of Hollywood and the celebrity leisure class.

The Magic of Opportunity

In his 1986 State of the Union Address, Ronald Reagan spoke of the "magic of opportunity—unreserved, unfailing, unres-trained—isn't this the calling that unites us?" Reagan's oracular visions appealed to our nostalgic belief in magic—the kind of magic that the enterprising individual can use to create prosperity. He appealed to our sense of calling to the religion of business as the economic elect that will be rewarded for our effort in using magic to create the cornucopia of wealth that is the promise of American capitalism. This belief is rooted in popular economics, the folklore and fable of the prosperity of the Town. The romantic heroism of the entrepreneur and the inventor was a result of their adherence to the canons of popular economic lore. Americans were called to prosper through the proper forms of faith and ritual and could not be denied their right to the blessings of election. This has been complemented by the romantic heroism of consumption, the legitimacy of enjoying the rituals of self-indulgence. Economic orthodoxy in a recrudescent Age of Business had nostalgic roots, but also contemporary justifications in the popular leisure class that the Reagans headed. Guided by the unity of moral and material orthodoxy, we responded to the mythic lure of the god of prosperity.

Americans have often been accused of reducing freedom to the freedom to make and spend money. This is not entirely true, but our wish to exalt business activity and the orthodoxies of popular economics to quasi-religious status in periods such as the Age of Reason does seem to identify freedom with wealth. This was no more evident than in the rededication ceremony for the Statue of Liberty on July 3-4, 1986, over which Reagan presided. The Goddess of Liberty, wrote Gorer,

is America the bountiful, pouring out endless treasures from her cornucopia. She is America the Land of the Free, holding high her torch to illuminate the path to democracy for the benighted. She is America the Land of Opportunity, yielding her favors to those who are industrious, energetic, and ingenious enough to deserve them. (51-52)

Yet the elaborate and garish ritual extravaganza celebrating the refurbishing of Miss Liberty as a national symbol was more a celebration of power than freedom. The cost of the work on the statue was borne largely by the tax-deductible donations of the wealthy and corporations, who were rewarded by the status of official sponsors, using the Liberty symbol in their advertising. Those on Governor's Island the night Reagan "relit" Liberty paid handsomely for the privilege; there were no tired, poor, or huddled masses. Liberty stood for the ascendancy of wealth and the sovereignty of business in a gigantic commercial civilization. Some critics even saw the Liberty show as a smug appropriation of a national symbol of freedom by the rich and mighty as a self-conscious justification for their power. Certainly the ceremony included the mytheme of material exceptionalism, that our own laws of popular economics were still valid and that we were exempt from the shifting tides of economic history as long as we abided by the basics.

The tone of the pseudo-event was elegiac, since it occurred precisely at a time when immigration was a threat and not a promise, when liberty was being diminished and not expanded and when economic power was shifting elsewhere. It was an invocation of magic to recapture our exceptionalism in an era of declining belief in progress, and indeed the entrepreneurial ideal itself. Reagan himself urged our faith more in the magic of technology than the magic of enterprise, a shift away from belief in man (the "spirit of capitalism" of popular economics) to belief in technology (the blind power of machines of popular mechanics). With those threatening processes at work, appeals to the magic of material exceptionalism should have been expected. The Old Colossus of Reagan's America was no longer a golden door, but a bastion of power to be defended against history. The theme of restoration and preservation of Miss Liberty was significant, symbolized by the slogan of the U.S. Treasury advertisements selling commemorative coins: "Let's Keep Liberty in Mint Condition—Forever," as if Liberty had to be remembered as unspoiled and thus could not be used.

Ceremonies such as the Statue of Liberty celebration cast Reagan as the Boy Mayor of the national Town conducting rituals of business, magical invocations of the myth of eternal prosperity. It is a long way from the store-front businesses of Dixon to the international corporation, but the necessity of magical origins and latter-day representation remained crucial. Nostalgic politics hoped to overcome the gap between the diminutive scale of Town business and the giganticism of the Fortune 500, the potential Scroogeism of acquisitive capitalism (such as Potter in *It's a Wonderful Life*) and the Reaganesque myth of capitalism as an altruistic and philanthropic enterprise, the retention of moral rectitude in prosperity without descent into consumptive antinomianism. Further, the myth of capitalist benevolence could only persist if we continued to believe in Reagan as an economic authority, someone who convinced us that the magic of opportunity could be obtained from Town to Multinational. The stock market crash of 1987 may have dampened our belief in the eternity of capitalist prosperity and the fundamental soundness of the economic theology Reagan evoked. But it did little to undermine Reagan's renewed heroic attempt to elevate the profane to the realm of the sacred, reminding Americans of their true faith and worship.

Chapter Four
The Church

In The Town, the Family went to Church. The popular order of Town and Nation was sustained and blessed by obeisance to God. Moral and material prosperity was a product of the democratic social contract of which God was a partner. The Church supported the legitimacy of the other secular institutions of The Town, providing the moral basis of civil consensus of value and action. The Town was enjoined never to forget the familiar mystery of its own blessing, and thus its duty to God's Church. The minister was a cultural archetype of social responsibility, reminding The town, the Family and the Business of its commitment to the popular order. In the nostalgic image, The Church held a special place in the institutional mix and imbued Town and Nation with divine sanction. The fact that they were and increasingly are secularized, and that religion has been relegated to a special and limited place in the popular order, has not prevented the re-emergence with Reagan of a claimed identity of God and Government. Like Andrew Jackson, there was a temptation on the part of the ardently religious to see the romance of the hero's quest as one with Nation and God, redeeming Nation and serving God's Will.

Americans have always been a religious people, and the theme of God's exceptional favor has been a cultural theme from the start. In our imagined nostalgic order, there was an easy blend of the sacred and secular, with the bourgeois social contract held together by the glue of godliness. The Stewart-figure as social and political leader was so partly because of his acceptance of popular piety (George Bailey, after all, had been saved for his social role by God) and rejection of popular impiety (as in *King's Row*, impiety seemed to follow disaster around). The weekly round of pietistic rituals gave magical sanction to The Town: grace at every meal, prayer in school, prayer to start the businessman's or lodge's meeting, Bible reading at home, church socials and of course Sunday. The will

103

to believe in God's blessing at the outset had been a work of political creationism, and that will had to be constantly re-created in order to remind us of the "new sacred order" of The Town.

Ronald Reagan could not be identified clearly with any particular sectarian group, but religious folk and eminent divines could identify him as a nostalgic agent of the national religion drawn from The Town of the mythic past, with God becoming somehow "ours" as a nation. As Ward noted, "Perhaps the most durable among the many ideas that have fallen under the generic term, nationalism, is the belief that God will see to it that America will succeed." In such an atmosphere and with such beliefs uniting transcendent and national principles and purposes, it is no wonder that a particular politician can come to be seen in the popular mind as an agent of God's will, since after all he represents in his political personage the unity of the will of God and the will of the people. Yet, there was in this easy identity of God, nation and leader, something potentially blasphemous and politically dangerous, for such identity elevated America to a predestined march to glory and thus elevated her politics—including her foreign policy—to a divinely sanctioned purpose; it gave the nation the sense that material and moral prosperity are God's gift for our solicitude and thus not other people's; and it meant that a particular leader could gain great power by representing himself as "God's select instrument" who mediates between God and the democratic folk who believe in Him, and him (Ward, *Andrew Jackson* 110-14).

We have argued that nostalgia serves us in the present as a statement of faith. We wished to have faith in both a sacred and secular destiny, so we imagined a unity of origins in which there was no tension between church and state. Reagan came to represent not only the cult of the state, but also the cult of the church, that because of its "special place" in the American Town, the church—the patriotic and conservative church—should be accorded privilege. Reagan's metachurch was nondenominational and nonsectarian, held together by appeal to national mythology rather than the logical agreement. The Town had been the creation of divine blessedness for the special mission America had been chosen for, becoming the seedbed for communal religion. Metareligion acted as a "sacred canopy" for the Town, as moral guardian of the institutional consensus. In the Age of Reason, the myth of religion fulfilled the purposes of nostalgic politics, giving sacral legitimacy to the worship of state and leader. In that way, it served the imperial function of public veneration of the political gods.

Reagan as Godsend

Reagan came to political power in the wake of one of the recurrent outbursts of American religiosity, during what Tom Wolfe called the "Third Great Awakening." This was a period of moral poverty in the wake of the burst of political and hedonistic energy and liberation during the 1960s, and the subsequent search for personal salvation during the disillusioned and narcissistic 1970s correctly named "the 'Me' Decade" (Wolfe). It was perhaps inevitable that there would be a spiritualistic reaction from this period of rapid change and moral drift, seeking some kind of transcendental explanation and solace in a world that seemed to make less sense. When the cultural "moral self" is set adrift, there is an attempt to redefine one's identity by reference to a variety of symbols, some of which are religious, so we should have expected the growth of cults, "new age" philosophies and religions, and most importantly, conversions to evangelical groups.

If, in 1980, the "stage was set for the entrance of a heroic figure as President, a man on a white horse, by the sense of impending disaster in the country and by performance and persona of Carter," much of this "sense" stemmed from the fear of moral disaster (Fisher 302). A parent, preacher, or pundit could read the statistics and view with alarm what they believed was happening. For those people that envision America as a "redeemer nation," the 1970s were evidence that we had gone too far towards the consequences of the "secular city" or the "naked public square" wherein our original missionary righteousness has been dissipated by the hedonistic corruptions of the present (Neuhaus). In such an atmosphere, the political stage was set for the emergence of a figure from romantic democracy and not a pragmatic man of the present, a figure who was seen by some at least as "God's select instrument."

Like all politicians, Reagan confessed shamelessly to his belief in and dependence upon the Almighty. In the volume of his "letters," in one chapter entitled "The Spirit of the Man," we learn that Reagan was "unabashedly moral and deeply religious" and "has a strong belief that the Lord's will plays a part in the affairs of men and that faith in the Lord is essential if a man is to achieve great things." "I have come to realize," he wrote in 1976, "that whatever I do has meaning only if I ask that it serves His purpose" and hoped as President he would "serve God." Reagan's theological positions coincided nicely with his politics: churches should not coerce government to redistribute wealth, taking prayer out of public schools helped cause the decline of discipline and SAT scores, welfare should be based on "voluntary" Christian desire to help others and not governmental action, and that because of the welfare state "with the best of intentions, with only a desire to help those less fortunate, we are making a god of government." He stated his belief in providential geography: "I have long believed there was a divine plan that placed this land here to be found by people of a special kind that we have a rendezvous with destiny." He displayed his belief in the magic of romantic democracy by a nostalgic belief in an earlier "Christian America" and a call to return to those principles of moral and material prosperity by saying:

I am deeply concerned with the wave of hedonism—the humanist philosophy so prevalent today—and believe this nation must have a spiritual rebirth, a rededication to the moral precepts which guided us for so much of our past, and we must have such a rebirth very soon.

Indeed, such faith has been in the past a guarantor of international peace:

If you will look back at the periods of the longest peace in our country you will find they have been those times when the United States based its international decisions and relations on sound moral principles with the firm expression that rather than sacrifice such principles we would fight.

If, then, we "return to the morals of a Christian society," Divine Providence will reward again a "nation under God" with the just rewards given the faithful in the imagined peaceable kingdom of the mythic past (van Damm 88-98).

By 1980, Reagan's nostalgic restatement of the mytheme of Divine blessing on an America that is faithful, and Divine wrath on an America that has strayed, found response in many religious circles. Many religious folk used to think of show biz and Hollywood people as representations of modernistic immorality, hedonistically living the high life depicted in the movie fanzines and thus as dangerously alluring threats to conventional grassroots values.

Further, the more ardent among his religiously oriented followers were puzzled by Reagan's casual attitude toward religion. He was raised in the Disciples of Christ church, but during his years in Hollywood was never noted for religious devotion. His theological stances as Governor and President were vague, generalized, sentimental and non-sectarian. Eminent divines on the Christian Right fretted that they didn't even know if Reagan was truly "born again," since he apparently never had had an electrifying conversion experience, and defined himself as being born again by the fact that once he was "voluntarily baptized." The church he attended (but didn't join) in Bel Air was not intensely sectarian and the minister, the Reverend Moomaw, was more a figure of Hollywood than of Liberty Mountain. Perhaps most astonishing was the fact that Reagan rarely attended church, with the slightly suspect excuse that he didn't want to embarrass fellow parishioners with all the security precautions they would have to go through. So he spent Sunday morning at home. Despite the campaign propaganda film scene where he recalled saying after he was shot that "whatever time I have left belongs to Him," Reagan's "personal" relationship to Him remained frustratingly vague to the faithful who wanted desperately to believe in him as an agent of Him.

For many of the religious Right, Reagan was nothing less than a godsend. He was the first President in recent memory who represented their values and their social agenda in the White House and gave them hope that they could recreate a mythic "Christian America." In a society and political system that seemed to many of them to be drifting toward secular values and hedonistic practices they didn't like, Reagan appeared as a romantic hero who espoused social policy and theological grounding of that policy from the Presidential pulpit. Indeed, in one version of his ascent to power, Reagan was anointed by God. In an unofficial but obviously laudatory campaign biography in 1984, Reagan is pictured as a man of great faith and Christ-like forbearance and rectitude. But more, God has spoken to believers of his anointment. In the biography, the born-again author recounts that in 1970 Reagan and his wife met with a small group of lay evangelists and clasped hands in a circle of prayer. One of them, a wealthy California businessman, began to sway and tremble and speak in tongues. As he became "filled with the spirit of the Lord," the businessman prophesized of Reagan: "If you walk uprightly before Me, you will reside at 1600 Pennsylvania Avenue." The businessman confirmed the incident by pointing out that "it was interesting that the Lord gave me his exact address" (Woodward and Bailey 30; Slosser).

It is likely that even his most fervent religious supporters would shrink from such a characterization, yet the process of political representation of deeply held symbolic values often involves projecting attributes and destinies on the representer that gives them an exalted and quasi-sacred status. A search for a satisfying aesthetic reality in an incoherent universe often coheres around an individual hero who represents the quest in his or her personage. By representing transcendent values on a political stage, the hero acquires the magic and myth of those values and thus becomes himself an agent of transcendence. The danger, of course, is that such identification translates into demands for uncritical support of the romantic hero and a hope that he enforces monistic values. For some, when they heard the term "Christian America," all they saw was barbed wire. But there are all kinds of culturological currents in American society that mitigate against such monistic integration under an anointed leader that would have to be overcome for such a "barbed wire" historical outcome to triumph. Indeed, ironically again, Reagan represented some of these antimonistic currents too.

American Popular Religiosity

Here we may make a distinction between "religiousness" and "religiosity." The former involves a sincere relationship between a person and transcendent values, often personal and pietistic, but perhaps more often involving some public, group-related confession of faith. The latter involves the use of religion for some social purpose other than the individual's (or group's) search for religious truth. Religiosity is only quasi-religious, invoking religious values for purposes other than religiousness. To be sure, religiousness on the part of at least a segment of society is a prerequisite for social religiosity. But the purpose of celebrations of religiosity is not primarily religious but rather social. In other words, the function of occasions of social religiosity serve culturological and not theological purposes. If conducted properly, a social occasion of religiosity is not sectarian, although it may be conducted by sectarian groups. It is not theocentric but rather homocentric, celebrating not the individual's or church's link to God but rather their link to society (Hart 98). Often such occasions are social rituals, conducted by authorities drawn from church, social group, or politics designed to celebrate the power and rectitude of the relationship of religion and society.

In the United States, the pluralistic range of religious beliefs combined with the formal separation of church and state has resulted in a wide range of rituals of *political religiosity*. Everything from invocation by ministers at local high school football games to Presidential inaugurals shows Caesar's obeisance to God, a vaguely defined and certainly nonsectarian God who blesses everything American, from high school football players to Presidents. Such political rituals are tepid and obligatory moments, something that football players and Presidents suffer through as part of their public duty before they can crack heads or invade countries. Yet the recurrent recrudescence of religious belief and organizations in a highly secular and "rational" society dictates ritual recognition and rhetorical celebration.

In its most august form, Americans speak of "high church" political religiosity as our civil religion, the ritual and rhetorical obeisance that political leaders pay to religious values. In national rituals of pomp and circumstance—a regular ritual such as a Presidential inaugural or an occasional ritual such as a Kennedy funeral of 1963—the rhetorical integration of religious and political symbols is quite high, although afterwards it is business as usual for both politicians and prelates as they return to their respective dominions. But in these moments, the profane world of government pays homage to the world that is sacred. This ritual relationship is given various names—"civic piety," "religious nationalism," "public religion"—but in America it amounts to symbolic association of the civil order with religious sanction in an exercise of political religiosity.

However, the grassroots mind takes the exercise of religiosity a step further than political and religious elites. Religiosity is an organic part of the common life of American existence. In the bourgeois culture of suburb and small town, ethnic neighborhood and retirement community, religion is part of people's social rounds and thus is "rationalized" in terms of the way Americans live. Religious values serve the beliefs and lifestyles of such lives, rather than the other way around. If people hold economic and political values, religion in America tends to adjust to those mainstream social values. Too, churches are institutions that serve a variety of other social functions, such as weddings, picnics, softball and so on. For this reason, American grassroots religion has lost a lot of its raw and fervid backwoods intensity, as Americans since the Depression have come to be elevated to and participate in bourgeois culture. As polls indicate, there is still a lot of religiousness out there, although tempered even in evangelical circles by the material prosperity of American middle-class life.

For these reasons, the common life of Americans includes popular religiosity, the use of religion at the grassroots level for a wide variety of social functions. This can range from the relatively innocuous (prayer at a Rotary breakfast) to the downright blasphemous. In the latter case, perhaps the most discomfiting for sincere Christians is easy association of Christianity with business values and Chamber of Commerce boosterism. Such identity has seen much popular expression going back to the Horatio Alger books, Russell H. Conwell's "Acres of Diamonds" lecture and, of course, Bruce Barton. Barton, one of the pioneers of modern advertising, in *The Man Nobody Knows* (1924), used the Christian story as an exemplar for business—Jesus was the founder of modern business, a kind of holy salesman who sold a product to a disbelieving world by inspiring his disciples to be hustling traveling salesmen; that He was a great advertiser, and the crucifixion a great publicity stunt; and that He was a sociable hale-fellow-well-met who liked to party and have a good time; and that He was a real man, no weak sissy, that would appeal to sociable American businessmen. Sinclair Lewis' famous caricature Babbitt is a popular representation of business boosterism, a practitioner of "practical religion" who brought good business practices and advertising to boosting Sunday School attendance (Barton; S. Lewis).

Popular religiosity makes "practical religion" possible by making religious values and practices "fit into" the grassroots community. In this way, the church can avoid involvement in and espousal of issues that might be subversive to the institutional balance of the imagined community. Religiosity serves the mythic pattern of institutional ideas as exemplified in the small town of the popular mind. It is a mild and not fervent religion, is relatively non-sectarian and "untheological," and most importantly, is no threat to the array of power and wealth of the secular institutions it largely supports. In that sense, the church of Rockwellville is a creature of romantic democracy, a "practical religion" that is integrated into the secular society and legitimates the power exercised by secular institutions—family, business and school. In the American imagination of a past peaceable kingdom the church supports the power of the community by guiding it in the direction of moral and material prosperity.

This can be illustrated simply by reference to how much popular religion in America supports grassroots secular values such as optimism, voluntarism and gain. Americans really have very little sense of either sacred or secular tragedy or even pathos; for us "life is a happy thing, a promising thing, a thing wherein God is in His heaven and with Americans, too" (Furay 50). With our belief in progress, an American destiny that is foreordained by a benevolent God, it follows that much of American popular religion avoids the tragedy and suffering of religious faith for the more upbeat theme of how religion offers hope, and that the lesson of religious hope means that secular life should be lived with inspired effort. This optimism of popular religiosity interweaves with grassroots capitalist values, generally supporting norms of personal achievement and possessive individualism. Much of popular religion finds little tragedy in greed; to the contrary, much rhetoric of religiosity still links God and gold in an optimistic alliance of "the gospel of wealth."

Although he had many predecessors, the post-World War II figure who most successfully linked popular Christianity with capitalist success was Norman Vincent Peale. Peale became a popular religious figure in the 1950s by his promulgation, in new form and through new media, of a very old American fantasy: that if one cultivates the proper religious, moral and work attitudes, one's success is guaranteed. Peale was in the grand tradition of the American achievement ethic, his "power of positive thinking" message gave a religious justification for capitalist success. Indeed, religious belief became a major source of one's success. Peale's popular sermons carried the old gospel of wealth into the postwar world. Like many other more recent "self-help" messages, it included the narcissistic principle of psychological rewards as well as material rewards accruing from the individualistic cultivation of self-development.

Peale's principle of positive thinking has had many recent copies and variants such as Robert Schuller's "possibility thinking." The more secular self-help books of the 1970s were variations on the theme, positing the achievement of sexual success, psychological balance, organizational ascendancy, physical health, or simply crass accumulation of power and money. Some TV clerics made a direct equation between qualities of religious faith and the appearance of cash. The "positive principle" was celebrated precisely by those most in need of reassurance that business success was deserved, and it indeed even possessed an odor of sanctity. Peale was important because he revived in a new age religious approval for capitalist activity. Not only achievement but success was given again the original Protestant sense of godly activity, a sign of favor. Peale was the modern godfather of self-help and remained the "guru" of the Rotarians. His political conservatism was the mild Midwestern Babbitry, not the flaming Manicheanism of the fundamentalists. He helped to refurbish the optimistic gloss to an ideology in question even among the people who had benefited by it. Peale gave a latter-day popular impetus to American boosterism, especially in its small town and small business setting.

If the equation between Christian and capitalist success seemed too much of a popular celebration of the essential unity of religious and economic optimism, this was tempered by an uncritical call on the part of churches for secular voluntarism in helping solve community problems. This was a popular demonstration of the essential unity of church and business, in which the former institution was to support the latter in the myth of capitalist benevolence, wherein the potentially anarchic individualism of possessive accumulation is tempered by Christian values that makes the business a responsible and legitimate member of the community.

The popular religiosity of the grassroots mind mutes the potential conflicts between the Christian church and Main Street by mutual cooperation in negotiating the "contract" of local self-government. The widespread mass commitment to religiousness is watered down by the secular influence of religiosity, which takes the critical sting out of the sacred view of the profane. And conversely, the influence of the church tempers the sterner strictures of the classical business ideology of social Darwinism, which in its meanest form cast businessmen into the role of Ebenezer Scrooges who complain about the taxes they pay for the poor. The ethos of rugged individualism and savage competition is muted by encompassing "free enterprise" with the Christian ethic of service and social good; the prosperity of the entrepreneur is given religious sanction, since according to the social vision of popular religiosity, business prosperity is good for the community as a whole. This religious sanction is very different from the older undercurrent in Protestant thought that business prosperity is a sign of God's favor and thus one's election and salvation; rather it is a sanction that business prosperity is a sign of community favor and in return business owes support to the other organic institutions that constitute the town. Since charity is a product of capitalistic prosperity, business integrates nicely with the moral prosperity of the community that created it.

The local church is crucial in providing the support of business, even if that makes its theology more a product of the *Reader's Digest* than *Revelation*. Popular religiosity dictates a kind of uncritical banality on the part of local churches that tempers on the one hand disturbing theological messages (such as sermons about how difficult it is for rich men to enter the Kingdom of Heaven) but on the other civilizes the potential barbarities of social Darwinism. Such a "contract" developed in the history of local self-government in America in part to control the potential of anarchic individualism on the part of the urban and industrial equivalent of the Man of the West, the "robber baron" business buccaneer of the heroic days of nineteenth-century capitalism unrestrained by a sense of social responsibility for his success. As we have seen, the Man of the West is pagan and savage, someone who is heroic but also bad for business, garden clubs and churchgoing. So too was the robber baron, whose unbridled ambition and greed gave them such power that they seemed more like feudal than democratic lords. But in the nostalgic model of the democratic community, the businessman had to be made safe for the community and conversely the community safe for him. The compromise of the grassroots mind was popular religiosity, which made the businessman not only a supporter of family life and local education, but also made him a churchgoing man, a deacon civilized and housebroken by the force of Christian life. Like Scrooge, the businessman was made into a supporter of the "feminine" virtues that guided the other institutions of the town: charity, culture, recreation, "society." One could see this developing in the formation and activities of community-oriented clubs— Chambers of Commerce, Lions, Rotary, Optimists and so on.

Popular morality here was more a matter of social sanction than religious dogma, and churches were less adept at producing saints than "good citizens" (Furay 83-4). Many of those good citizens were men of business, whose financial and personal support of the church was reciprocated by the ideological support of the institution, largely precluding any potential conflict between the sacred and profane. Business vocation was given sacred sanction, and the myth of capitalist benevolence was celebrated in the "voluntarism" expected of the churchgoing businessman, backed by a theology of good works rather than faith. Indeed, an enduring theme in popular culture has been the businessman who quietly and even anonymously voluntarily does good works with his own money. We are reminded of Lloyd C. Douglas' 1950s novel *Magnificent Obsession*, which deals with a playboy turned doctor, who through romantic love and a non-denominational religious commitment, helps the needy and refuses public credit or payment. This was consistent with Reagan's—and perhaps the vast majority of American businessmen's—conviction that charity should be voluntary and private, based on a belief in the idea that charity should be a product of private religiosity.

Nowhere is the essential culturological unity of grassroots institutions more evident than in the seasonal rituals of Christmas. It is, after all, the "spirit of Christmas" that somehow transforms Scrooge from a skinflint social Darwinist into, vaguely, a more altruistic and warmhearted "Christian." In Ronald Reagan's America, Christmas remained the most important national seasonal ritual, combining economic, political and religious symbols in cultural rites of self-congratulation. But in grassroots America, the seasonal celebration of Christmas has a lot more to do with national than religious symbolism. True, there are expressions of religiousness on the part of the devout, but much more common, and important, are the expressions of religiosity. Typical of the latter are the semi-mandatory rituals of the family gathering during the holiday season. At such gatherings, there may be religious observance—praying over the turkey or attending a Christmas Eve service—but the central focus of this familial drama is in the display of prosperity through the exchange of gifts and the consumption of food and drink. Indeed, much of the American economy is geared to buying at Christmas time, and after the holiday season the figures of the orgy of consumption are studied as an augur to the health of the economy. Both political and religious figures celebrate our national prosperity at this season, linking our wealth to God's favor for our submission to Him. It is obligatory for the First Family to gather, announce what they give each other, have the Christmas dinner and so forth in ritual leadership of the common rites held in millions of households around the land. Every Christmas as President, Reagan would be televised offering his Christmas message to the nation.

But what of the poor, the homeless, the lonely during this period? They of course were a troublesome lot, not sharing in the warm glow of the national rite of self-congratulation. But consciences could be momentarily salved by a variety of church-sponsored charity drives before the holiday season, assuring that the wretched of the land did have a soup-kitchen Christmas dinner, that children of the unemployed would have presents and that the lonely would have a volunteer companion. Then, after a few tepid calls for the "spirit of giving" to continue the year around, the outsiders of the rites of national self-congratulations are "taken care of" and quickly forgotten. Such a ritual serves important functions of popular religiosity, including ritual reassurance of the justice of the distribution of wealth, the legitimacy of opulent consumption and the religious sanction given to grassroots institutions. Local churches lead this rite of national religiosity, but it serves to celebrate the material as well as the moral prosperity of the bourgeois majority. Such a rite utilizes politico-cultural "magic," invoking supernatural powers to "bless" us through a seasonal ritual that demonstrates once again our essential unity and goodness and the myth of capitalist benevolence.

Reagan represented these themes in American popular religiosity and celebrated the rites of political religiosity, such as the observance of Christmas, as political leader of the country. This was the Reagan of the White House Christmas tree lighting; of his Christmas call, in the depths of the recession of 1982, for the nine of us who were working to look after the one who wasn't (unemployment was above 10%); of declaring 1983 National Bible year; of calling for every church in America to voluntarily adopt ten poor families; of the non-sectarian practical religion of the Rotarians and Peale; of God the "Genial Philanthropist" who blesses America with her deserved bounty. This is the grassroots image of a religion that offers civic and moral lessons but offers no revelatory message that interferes unduly with the conduct of the common life. "It is now a sociological and historical truism," wrote Conrad Cherry, "that any religion which becomes a vital part of its culture is inclined to maintain the status quo of that culture. When the motifs of the national faith are invoked, therefore, it is frequently for the sake of uncritical endorsement of American values and tasks" (Hart 80). This side of Reagan's political piety was in this rhetorical tradition of invoking the "help of God" for our common national and individual values and tasks without conjuring up theological themes that might interfere with legitimate pursuits.

The Inspiration Industry

The rise of Reagan to power in the 1980s was augured by the popular movements of the 1970s dubbed "the Me Decade" (Wolfe). This emergent "hardline" culture of narcissism revived the ancient American myth of anarchic individualism with a new vengeance, applying the ethos of autonomous self-help to a wide variety of areas of endeavor. The nostalgic American call for "self-reliance," "rugged individualism" and "autonomy" was given new impetus. After the failure of the communitarian and egalitarian impulses of the 1960s, the reactionary populism of the 1970s extolled an individualist ethic. If it is the case that Americans vacillate between the contradictory values of equality and achievement then in the Age of Reason the achievement myth was ascendant. But in an age of economic and social uncertainty, the individuals felt left to their own devices and were thus attracted to the mythology that impelled and justified their belief in their own will to succeed.

"Popular Pealism" was the source of legitimation. Rather than the virgin land dream of the first frontiers and the industrial dream of the heroic era of capitalism, the new frontier is a dream of psychological riches, i.e., that one's *attitude* makes a difference not only in one's private happiness but also in one's social happiness, of which work is simply one part. Popular religion in America was the culturological source of this ideological union. Books such as *Looking Out for No. One, Ambition,* W. Clement Stone's *Success through a Positive Mental Attitude* and so forth were in the tradition of offering readers the secular dream of material success through individual initiative. The latter-day fantasy of success is "guaranteed" by the cultivation of the right attitude, which the psychological disposition of some form of "niceness" usually becomes the key to success.

The religiously-derived contemporary rhetoric of success serves a larger popular function than the secular success literature. The latter courted the danger of justifying ruthless selfishness and powerseeking, such that the American self-conception of local community could not tolerate. Secular power had to be reconciled once again with religion, and it was here that popular Pealism played a legitimating role. Social necessity led to the creation of what we may call the "inspiration industry," those who gave godly sanction to secular institutions and more basically linked religious inspiration with the psychological attitudes that motivate people to strive for secular success. The phrases from Peale's rhetoric communicate the ideas that recur from this industry: "positive thinking," "in-depth faith," "the excitement principle" and so on. Television divine Robert Schuller updated the same inspirational message with his "possibility thinking." Perhaps the most colorful of the "motivational speakers" of the period, who made the compromise between God and gold seem easy, was Zig Ziglar who once said:

Every once in a while, some of my Christian brothers will come up to me, do a fast halo adjustment, and say, "How do you reconcile all that talk about money with Christianity?" And I'll say, "It's easy. I believe God made the diamonds for *His* crowd, not Satan's bunch." (qtd. in Friedman 24)

The inspiration industry of the 1970s and 1980s was a secular theology that emphasized the ancient American fantasy that individual will could triumph over social structure, by recommending not the ruthless will of the robber baron but rather the will of the nice guy whose gladhanding hustle, ability to get along with the old boys and example of motivation and enthusiasm wins the day. The image of the successful man is based not on the remote and forbidding Old Testament God of power and wrath, but rather the popular image of Jesus as your buddy, an easygoing pal who you get to know in a "personal" way and who sells you on his product by being your friend and catering to your secular desires. In this way Jesus becomes a role model figure easily accessible to the grassroots mind, combining the mythology of individual initiative and drive guaranteeing success with the relaxed posture of the "social ethic" which mitigates the furies of ambition with the sociability and familiarity of small-town and small-business relationships.

The secular theology of popular religiosity united religion and secular institutions on the core attitude of popular optimism. This is not quite the optimism of the true believer who believes he or she is assured of divine salvation. Rather it is faith that the attitude of optimism hones both personality and will together in a "winning combination" that serves the individual well. Optimism is a key to the culturologic of the will to believe. Andrew Jackson, we may recall, knew "no such word as Fail" and was extolled as possessing the proper temperament for success, symbolizing the cultural belief that the cause of a man's success lay within himself. His successful career was interpreted to support the more general cultural myth that individual will can overcome structure. But the myth is not a raw Nietzschean will to power. It is rather a tamer optimism that nice guys finish first. Business needs the attitude of optimism to undergird the individual virtues of work (ambition, productivity, initiative) and the virtues of sociability (friendliness, joviality, humor) to make organized effort possible. Popular religiosity, then, serves important politico-cultural functions by offering a folklore that unites religious belief with secular activity in an alliance that provides motivation for, and eases the conscience of, the grassroots mind.

Reagan represented, both in personality and philosophy, the themes of this popular alliance. His unshakeable optimism continued firm even in the wake of economic and political catastrophes. He was the nice guy who finished first because he believed and practiced the optimism of the American creed of religious and economic progress. His attitude was "right": he saw America as one long Main Street where the virtues of business are legitimate and indeed produce the prosperity that allows the successful to extend a voluntary helping hand to those "who through no fault of their own" didn't make it. The "moral Main Street" of Reagan's vision attaches no evil or guilt to business, and on the contrary gives it is quasi-religious sanction. In the Era of No Doubts over which he presided, the secular theology of optimism found renewed salience and articulation. Not only Reagan's grassroots business philosophy but also his manner represented the recrudescence of social niceness as a key to success. He was successful because of his personality and will, which had the small-town flavor of boyish charm with both ease and confidence, content with one's lot but always looking for something to turn up, moving leisurely through life without ever seeming strained or grasping. Riches and fame follow such a personality that not only works but also is sociable. Reagan could represent in the popular mind the notion that he could have been a success at anything he wanted, real estate development, car dealership, executive management, just because of the way he was.

As the chief spokesman for political religiosity and the secular theology of optimism, Reagan was in a sense the leader of the national inspiration industry too. Pointing to both his example and his national faith, he argued that he and the many other democratic heroes of everyday life were proof positive that not only did the national system work but that it had godly sanction. As a latter-day version of the American Adam, Reagan could root that inspired optimism so crucial to national "recovery" in the myth of American innocence. Our popular virtue was intact, Reagan seemed to say, so all we needed to do was inspire the good folks of grassroots America to believe once again in the rectitude of our motives and the sanctity of our pursuits. He was a representation for the popular mind of the unity of politico-cultural inspiration, defined as the motivation of the will to believe that both sacred and secular obstacles could be overcome in the Adamic quest for moral and material prosperity. The national destiny was represented as both moral and material, and doubts about the wisdom or unity of this quest were buried in the rhetoric of political religiosity.

Inspiration is an ephemeral and fragile enterprise easily undermined by doubt. For this reason, the optimism of politico-cultural inspiration is complemented by the negation of negating, condemning negativism. From the point of view of grassroots popular Pealism, the Edenic possibilities of the American Town are not only in constant danger from Soviet aggression and European sophistication, but also from within by moral decay as evidenced by negativism. A negative attitude is a threat to the inspired attitude that is basic to the belief system that binds together the social contract of romantic democracy. The message of optimism and morality of the inspiration industry is inseparable: the moral fiber that supposedly undergirds the material order is rooted in the optimistic will to believe, and immorality can thus be equated with a negativistic will to disbelieve. There is from this perspective something wrong, and certainly something damaging, about those who view with alarm rather than point with pride. If this might seem to the outside observer a somewhat Pollyannish view, that was simply an indication to those who shared the Reaganesque vision that critical thinking was one of the causes of our moral problems that prevented progress.

This was a major theme in the Reagan era. "At the grass roots level," said Ziglar in 1979, "in the great middle class, they're saying enough is enough. They're saying we want moral responsibility. One of the roles I hope to play is to urge people to examine their political candidates for their integrity, their love of America, and their belief in the free enterprise system" (qtd. in Friedman 30). In the 1984 campaign, Vice President Bush attacked Democratic opponent Walter Mondale for his "negative attitude," which made the election a choice between "The Great Communicator" (Reagan) and "The Great Depression" (Mondale). Bush went on:

The country is not like Mr. Mondale and Ms. Ferraro have characterized it. We are moving forward. There's still a lot to be done, but there are blue skies out there. And I just checked with the meteorologist, Mr. Mondale. The future is bright— just the opposite of what they tell us. (qtd. in *Chicago Tribune* sec. 1: 7)

Reagan's friend Walter Annenberg editorialized in his *TV Guide* in 1984 that there is

a new, optimistic spirit in America. . . . It is an optimism based on confidence that we *are* better off than we were four years ago, that we *can* find solutions to our problems, that our future *is* bright. . . [Reagan] personifies a strong, decent, forward-looking America. (Annenberg A3)

Such roseate rhetoric appealed to our nostalgia for an optimistic society where we saw nothing but blue skies, skies kept stormless by the invocation of politico-cultural magic that would revitalize the attitudes that inform individual self-reliance and add up to the re-creation of the religiously sanctioned social contract of local self-government.

But skeptics still wondered if this reassertion of the unified values of the nostalgic community could last. We may recall here the conclusion from Henry F. May's aptly titled "a study of the first years of our own time, 1912-1917," *The End of American Innocence*. That period was crucial in that it involved a crisis in

American values as exemplified in the pre-modern small town. Wilsonian Progressives exercised nostalgia for such an imagined place and hoped to initiate reforms that would restore the peaceable kingdom. Thus Progressivism had strains of reactionary populism and popular religiosity, but given the economic and social forces at work in the world, the embittering experience of World War I and the failure of Versailles, the Victorian and pastoral ethos of the nostalgic Dream could not be restored. May's conclusion about the Age of Wilson sounds hauntingly like the Age of Reagan. "In retrospect," he writes, "nostalgia comes easy. It is not hard to see the uses of unquestioned moral consensus in a world too shaken to be even rebellious." The civilization of 1912-20 failed as a result of "a permanent flaw in American nineteenth-century thought: its inveterate optimism. Peace, economic expansion and a large measure of general content were facts of the American scene most of the time. These had become confused with inevitable upward evolution and even with the coming of God's kingdom on earth...." Since then, "American civilization has been less happy, less unanimous and more precarious. On and off, it has also been more interesting. Its least successful periods have been those like the immediate present, times of false complacency that caricature the old confidence. Its best periods have been those when it has the most nearly come to terms with an unfriendly world." The end of American innocence, May concludes, was difficult for many since then to accept, "Those who look at it with dismay, or those who deny that, it happened, do so because they expect true stories to have a completely happy ending. This is a kind of innocence American history must get over" (H. May).

During his ascendancy to Presidential power, Reagan represented to his followers nostalgia for the imagined unity of moral and material values that was supposed to have existed in the past peaceable kingdom. He was a popular meta-authority who mediated the re-unification of those values in his Presidential present. But we may wonder whether the 1980s was a period of "false complacency that caricatured the old confidence," since the reunification of religious and business values was, after all, based on a mythical image and not the realities of American history. Business heroism still includes an element of heroism which finds religious devotion useful as "practical religion" supporting secular values. The easy optimism that characterized the Reaganesque

synthesis of moral and material prosperity ignored the dark agony
of religious belief far from the upbeat Babbitry of the Rotarians.
"One hears," wrote theologian Martin Marty, "the language of
kerygma, of apostolic proclamation, but it is as far removed from
the dread, despair, agony and brokenness of the cross as is the
diamond-cross jewelry in the cleavage of the nightclub performer"
(842). In a book on the religious broadcasters of the Reagan Era,
it is concluded that "for the broadcasters, it would appear that such
efforts as personal sacrifice, service, self-discipline, hard work,
setbacks, failures, and endurance are without theological
significance. God's presence is to be known only through benefit
and gain, toward which the viewer is continually prompted"
(Horsefield 46). The institutional alliance of sacred and secular may
have been theologically unsound, but is had culturological
resonance. For it reaffirmed that the American story was a true
story and that it would have a happy ending by the restoration
of the nostalgic model of local self-government with nothing but
blue skies all day long.

The imaginary state of The Town included the recrudescent
ideal of essential moral coherence in the American social contract.
Reagan re-affirmed the ease of the alliance and denied the existence
of dark conflicts between sacred and secular. The will to believe
does not exclude the secular will to succeed. Reagan not only claimed
mythic acquaintance with the timeless truths of popular order from
which we have fallen, as the iconic representation of the boy-mayor
of The Town, but also he extolled the eternal possibility of the
restoration of a popular morality that produced good and expunged
evil, recreating a G-rated society. In that way, Reagan was no
different than Grant, Harding, Coolidge, or Eisenhower—popular
Presidents who presided over metapolitical ages following great
social upheaval. The desire for bourgeois normalcy sanctioned by
a supportive church committed to reviving the myth of American
innocence may well be a "false complacency," but it did restore
the short-term if shallow optimism so essential to the will to believe.
Reagan re-ritualized for his constituency at least the "proper" status
and function of religion in the popular order: as the sacral support
for the American Town of happy endings.

Symbolic Crusade

The religious movements of the Reagan Era were not characterized solely by popular religiosity. If Reagan had celebrated only the traditional pseudo-alliance of business and religion, criticism and concern would have been limited to the traditional banality of the rhetorical relationship. But something else emerged from the popular movements of the time that not only helped elevate Reagan to power, but also made him flirt with the political dynamics of sectarian religiousness and not merely popular religiosity. As President, Reagan identified with and celebrated the religious symbols and social agenda of what came to be called the "Christian Right." By so identifying, it attracted to him the energies and enthusiasm of a social movement that became an electoral and lobbying force. For them, Reagan came to be the anointed representation of God's plans for America and the political agent of His agenda and His wrath. For all of his studied casualness about religion, Reagan became identified as no Presidential figure since William Jennings Bryan with a politics of popular redemption.

In the wake of the culture storm that swept the country in the 1960s, many people were faced with a value crisis, since the myth of American benevolence and essential social consensus was challenged. There was a wide variety of reactions to the cultural challenges of the 1960s and the disillusionments and drifts of the 1970s, not the least of which was a nostalgic desire for moral prosperity by re-integration into a moral community that vindicated one's moral self. The "culture of narcissism" in the 1970s was symptomatic of the moral malaise that affected the age. The "me first" self-indulgences of the time seemed to indicate that the anarchic individualism implicit in the material culture of consumption had run riot and that "doing your own thing" included indulging the most immoral sorts of desires. Not only did the American self seem to be identified with an orgy of consumption and hedonistic pleasures, but the pluralistic tolerance of behavior seemed to justify an ethic of "anything goes." The rise of cults, new age philosophies and religions, disco and punk rock, pornography and so on seemed to those who saw themselves as guardians of traditional morality stark evidence of widespread moral decay and social decadence. The proliferation of lifestyles and narcissistic pursuits we may term "popular antinomianism," which sees virtually everything as legitimate individual self-expression without the onus of moral guilt or social responsibility. The consequences of such unlimited tolerance conjured up fears of the cultural self being undermined in an orgy of Dionysian pursuits. The cultural will to believe became a powerful centripetal force that attempted to re-institute the conformity necessary for social order. William James long ago recognized this tension when he remarked, "Americans like to believe in things. They'll believe in anything they can. They would believe in everything if they could." Believing in anything and everything, however, takes the tradition of tolerance to the extremes, and thus the institutional order reasserted the nostalgic model of a past moral order in which there was consensus on popular morality.

In America, that nostalgic vision of a past moral order is rooted in the town church. Indeed, it may be the case that every moral order requires the legitimation of transcendent values. As Peter Berger asserted:

If one imagines oneself as a fully aware founder of society, a kind of combination of Moses and Machiavelli, one could ask oneself the following question: How can the future continuation of the institutional order, now established ex nihilo, be best insured? . . . . Set up religious legitimations. (33)

And as a society changes and there comes to be a period of perceived moral change and decay, the moral order can reassert itself by popular religious relegitimation. This is done through the mythic reassertion of the beliefs underlying the institutional order and by the conduct of a religiously based social movement that moves to enforce the model for social order through public policy. We are speaking here of something more aggressive and dynamic than the institutional contract of business and church at the local level; rather here we are observing a *symbolic crusade*, rooted in traditional morality and aimed at restating and re-instating the status of those morals. The political drama of status politics exalts certain values and degrades other values, usually by supporting some public figures and policies that further the desirable values and by scapegoating other public figures and policies that are believed to further undesirable values. As Gusfield argues, "governments function as representatives of the total society. . . . Much of the effective acceptance of government as legitimate rests upon the supposition that it is representative of the total society, that it has the moral responsibility 'to commit the group to action or to perform coordinated acts for its general welfare' " (168). Such a symbolic crusade seeks political representations of popular moral values, both in the representative's public lifestyle and his or her public stance with the movement.

The Christian Right became such a social movement in the 1970s and 1980s and found their political representative in Ronald Reagan. They had come to believe that government's toleration of popular antinomianism in the years since the 1960s was a threat to their definition of the traditional moral Self imagined in the nostalgic model of the American town. They sought someone who could mediate in his public personage the values they wished to further, and scapegoat those villains and fools who allegedly had brought us to this extreme of tolerating "alternative lifestyles." Jimmy Carter in particular drew their contempt for not sharing their moral fervor for a crusade against social evils. Even given his lifestyle and "beautiful people" connection, Reagan represented for them a Presidential figure drawn from that nostalgic moral past, and who espoused the return to "moral starch" that would transform the country's moral and material prosperity. For the rhetoric of both Reagan and the Christian Right made the bold claim not only that God blesses America, but that He has ceased by do so lately because of our moral decay; therefore, with the restoration of the godly moral values of the nostalgic past to an exalted status again, and a government-supported crusade against immorality, God's favor would be manifest with the restoration of material prosperity. This theory of the business cycle has not found its way into most economic textbooks yet, but it had mythic plausibility to those imbued with the nostalgic model. Explanations of political economy can be based in popular theories of politico-cultural magic, in which God comes to be the "unseen hand" who manipulated the economy and gave us seven lean years or seven fat years according to our moral obedience to Him. The investiture of power and authority the Christian Right accorded Reagan thus went far beyond him simply being right on the issues; more, he was right with God, a moral agent who espoused from the Presidential pulpit the right religious values and their application to our lives. As a divinely ordained godsend, he then became an agent of popular political redemption, representing the American "divine right" for the symbolic crusade that aimed at religious relegitimation of national values.

The God of Power

Reagan personally seemed an unlikely agent of political redemption, but became such because he, more than any previous President, spoke the religious language of redemption and, indeed, apocalypse. The more ardent among the Christian Right wanted much more than just a symbolic crusade against foreign and domestic evils. They wanted their values honored by power, but they also wanted the "power of right" to triumph now over evil before it was too late. They sensed, as did Reagan, an urgency about the historical "lateness" of their times and felt, with Reagan, "that it was not too late." Thus there developed during the 1980s an elaborate fantasy about recreating a "Christian America" with an agenda to redeem American society and indeed the entire world. Religion would not only be relegitimated as the moral glue of The Town; sacral power would be melded with secular power. This is an overreach of the nostalgic model for some, but not for others, like Reverend Jerry Falwell, who saw himself in a very real crusade, a "holy war" to "lead the nation back to the moral stance that made America great....We want to bring America back...to the way were were." Greg Dixon, leading light of the "Moral Majority" saw the Federal Government as "The Beast," a thing of Satan, a secular monster that supports evil and must be resacralized by a leader who pits his godly authority against it: "America is ripe for leadership which is godly and biblical" and will "chain the Beast." Among many who did not share the vision of a moral drama led by the American Christian children of light, such a "sense of an ending," of an apocalyptic denouement with the representatives of Satan on Earth, augured a fanatical enforcement of a repressive moral authority that was "biblical" and even the welcome of a final Armageddon against the Evil Empire.

Reagan courted the "Christian vote" through evocation of the moral authority of the vaguely Protestant church in The Town, vowing to write the traditional values that inhered in The Church Militant into present policy and claiming general faith in the immediacy of the Church Triumphant. His stance against popular secularization, or from the Christian Right point of view modernistic desacralization, gave them a political ally who shared their romantic pessimism about secular progress, but also echoed a hopeful faith in a redemptive meld of past and future. He shared the hope of taming the demon of secularism and put the genie of hedonism engendered by the consumer economy back in the bottle of moral rectitude. The world had been "dis-enchanted," with secular forces at work that seemed to undermine the nostalgic model of popular order with religion at its center. Reagan became, for those who yearned for that imagined moral consensus, something of a mortal god—the representation of the god of power that promised moral guardianships and the resacralization of the State. He was the unofficial head of a "remoralization" movement, re-creating the enchanted world of The Town once again as a moral vision, a place devoid of the ills of late twentieth-century secularity. The imaginary state of popular order was a world of moral consensus even with the plural "church of your choice."

But even though Reagan espoused specific issues as part of the Christian Right's remoralization agenda, he maintained a modicum of political distance from the movement in order to maintain his position as high priest of a non-sectarian vision of the moral order. Reagan had not the temperament nor the talent to lead a movement that enforced a draconian cultural purification. Piecemeal reforms were aimed at the hope of making secularity more tepid and "restoring" religious authority to an honored place in the popular order. "Religion," Reagan declared in 1984, "needs defenders against those who care only for the interests of the State." But his own defense was limited by interests of State, namely the promotion of economic prosperity through ever-expanding consumption. The doctrine of American mission that Reagan represented for his time included godly sanction of secular power, economic and political power that was antithetical to the creation of a "Christian America." Reagan did not only represent himself as an icon of the native moral self of Puritan origin, but more broadly as the embodiment of the American Self, with all the value contradictions that implied. The vision of romantic democracy embraces a mythic identity that Emerson once called the "imperial self," the American heroic identity that has Puritan origins but moves easily in the material world of acquisition and manipulation and reconciles or ignores conflict between traditional and libertarian morality, private and public realms, the sacred and the secular. Reagan was often accused of being a hypocrite, working the crowds of the faithful for votes but not sharing their zeal nor their faith. But an imperial self has to have politically broad shoulders, broad enough to support the utilitarian individualism of secular power as well as the biblical mission of individual and national redemption. Reagan could articulate his symbolic affinity with a Christian agenda for national salvation, but could not enforce it without violating the dream of institutional consensus. In the wake of the increasing historical force of secularization he could only invoke the Canute principle and give orders to the secular waves for the benefit of the faithful.

This was not cynically done, but it did demonstrate the limits of Reaganism as a political force. The imperial self as a political representation tries to include everybody, and thus can only appeal to American innocence, refusing to admit contradictions. If Reagan was an embodiment of American innocence, he was so as a cultural idealogue and not as a Grand Inquisitor. He did represent his age's expressed desire for cultural orthodoxy, but even his celebration of that had an elegiac quality to it, as if the "lateness" of the day had made us irredeemable. The nostalgic elegy for the centrality of popular religion revered an ideal that had lost its certain connection with broader moral and social purposes. As the world of the present becomes more disenchanted, nostalgic ceremonies of innocence had all the more appeal.

The American imperial self that Reagan represented has always been an astonishing bundle of contradictions. The grassroots mind encompasses both God and Mammon, the Puritan in Babylon, the sacred and the secular. Reagan mediated the contradictions for many among the religious (and not so religious) without overcoming them. The tension between the sacred and the secular has been there since the mythic beginnings of American culture and clearly will not be soon resolved simply by the symbolic celebration of the nostalgic model. Reagan was fond of quoting Puritan leader John Winthrop's "City on a Hill" sermon in 1620, in which he envisions a new and godly society "under a *due forme* of government both civil and ecclesiastical." But it is well to remember that Winthrop's godly city was a failure. "Massachusetts," observed Lawrence J. Towner,

failed as a Model of Christian Charity at the same time that it achieved worldly success: the generations which followed Winthrop's concerned themselves less and less with the perfection of souls and the achievement of salvation, and what had begun as a community dominated by religious purpose rapidly became a society with a secular orientation....Fifteen years after Winthrop's death, Roger Williams predicted: "Sir, when we that have been the eldest, and are rotting...a generation

will act, I fear, far unlike the first Winthrops and their Model of Love: I fear that
the common Trinity of the world (Profit, Preferment, Pleasure) will here be the
Tria omnia, as in all the world beside...that God Land will be (as it is now)
as great a God with us English as God Gold was with the Spaniards." (41)

The true moral majority in grassroots America lives easily with
waves of religious fervor as long as the profane quest for profit,
preferment and pleasure is not inordinately threatened; the American
empire is a secular society, and recrudescent protests of religiousness
and nostalgic calls for a return to our religious practices are answered
by celebrations of political religiosity which has not the intention,
nor the power, to return us to a Model of Christian Charity. The
politics of redemption does everything except redeem.

Reagan's power over the faithful, then, stemmed from his ability
to summon up a world of memory and illusion and to equate divine
and national purposes in an overarching world mission. He urged
us to come, love the beloved republic and God would bless America.
It was an empyrean vision that restored a popular metaphysic for
America's self-appointed mission in the world, but it appealed
because it seemed to emerge from Reagan's cultural omniscience,
his possession of and public espousal of the local knowledge of
romantic democracy. God would bless America again because of
our moral exceptionalism, and thus our innocent predestination,
in a world of otherwise power-exercising states. Reagan's power
to do more than assert this was severely circumscribed by those
power-exercising states (including the NATO countries), but it
satisfied his Christian following's will to believe in the imaginary
state of cultural orthodoxy and divine mission based on the "faith
of our fathers" to which we will be true, to death. Evil empires
are bested by righteous empires, and we know beforehand who will
win at Armageddon.

Reagan's play with Divine Right made him revered among
those anxious for the re-creation of a godly America, even if they
were frustrated by the recalcitrance of history to yield. Despite his
public theological confusion, his obeisance to the national authority
of God made him almost a mortal god himself, an indispensable
godsend who had saved the republic. Even though his actual power
was limited by secular history, Reagan had authority among the
faithful based on his representation of a popular metaphysic. Indeed,
his authority was cultural more than political, a meta-authority

that convinced and reassured but changed little. In any case, Reagan's authority was somewhat different than the famous typology of Max Weber. His authority was not based on tradition, but rather the dream-state of pseudo-history; it was not based on legal-rational authority, since that was the "disenchanted" world of secular power; nor was it really charismatic. Reagan appealed to tradition, to be sure, and used the legal-rational powers of the Presidency, but his cultural authority was elsewhere. He was often called "charismatic," but he claimed no gift of grace, founded no movement, nor brought radical change. He lived in a post-charismatic world that had every reason to fear charismatic authority based on fanatical devotion. Rather, his authority was oracular, which is not the same thing as charismatic. He was a popular oracle through which the deity speaks cultural and political truths, and who represented in his being cultural omniscience. An oracle has authority over opinion, but not action, not institutions and certainly not history. Oracular authority makes ritual statements of the hierarchy of truth and conducts ritual actions which celebrate the moral order sanctioned by God. Unlike the charismatic, the popular oracle cannot claim omnipotence, even for his own magical incantations; his authority is rooted in knowledge of an ideal world, not power over an actual one. Unlike traditional authority, the popular oracle succeeds because tradition has either been destroyed or denied; he must state again the discontinuous present's nostalgic image of a model universe. He stands above legal-rational authority as the possessor of a "higher truth" beyond the mundane squabbling of the moment; he is accorded wisdom because of his access to the kingdom of shadows that is the country of our minds.

Reagan's oracular status gave him a virtually unique opportunity to celebrate the link between God and government, church and state, past and future. He was, for example, the ritualistic head eulogist who presided over a succession of national funerals, reassuring us that dead Marines were "in God's loving arms" and that the Challenger crew had "touched the face of God." If the present was beyond redemption, the oracle could at least use the past as consolation: if we could but make the future the past, the peaceable Kingdom would be ours. But if the present proves to be irredeemable, the oracle can also offer us the consolation of prophecy, even if he is a prophet of doom. Reagan's repeatedly stated belief in the romance of apocalypse, of the "prophecies coming together" in our time, warmed the hearts of evangelicals who believed that the world was in the last days and that a nuclear Armageddon with the Soviet Union was both imminent and desirable.

An oracle is a religious seer of national destiny, and for Reagan to wonder "if we're the generation that is going to see [Armageddon] coming about" sounded uncomfortably like a self-fulfilling prophecy. Such an apocalyptic fantasy, innocent of hidden intention, was an oracular vision of the ultimate American mission in the world, to serve as God's vessel of wrath in the fulfillment of the providential drama of history. Reagan told the faithful that God was a national tribal deity who was in control of the world's destiny and that we might have the honor and duty to serve His apocalyptic Will, fulfilling His prophecy of the fire next time. This vision was playing with an apparently recrudescent myth of romantic apocalypse that emerged in the turmoil of the late twentieth century. The forces of evil were so strong, it was thought, that the judgment of God was imminent. Led by Reagan, many Americans saw themselves as the last bastion of Right and even as God's instrument in the Final Battle. With God on our side, we would inevitably win, the wicked would be punished and the oracular prophecy of god would be manifest. The romance of Revelation is combined with the American sense of destiny in godly purpose.

Reagan's musings about the contemporary religious "sense of an ending" were countered by the awful prospect of nuclear destruction. But believing that the Soviets were the Antichristic "focus of evil" in the world led to only one other alternative: to shield the Peaceable Kingdom with an impregnable defense that prevented attack from without and impose the orthodoxies of The Church in order to remoralize the popular order. Both ideas were romantic visions, appealing to the recurrent strain of popular isolationism and moral guardianship. And both emerged in the oracular authority of Reagan because of the inability of the godly and the patriotic to control change.

History and human frailty are beyond the power of even a mortal god to stop. Oracles speak the language of ritual truths, not historical processes. Those ritual truths made Reagan the oracle of cultural omniscience for the faithful. But it could not make him, nor the godly and moral order of fantasy, omnipresent. The oracle would not always be there to speak of worlds beyond.

Chapter Five
The Country

Ronald Reagan presided over the celebration of an imaginary country, one rooted in the mythography of a people undergoing rapid social change and historical displacement. The Town is at the core of the great American Interior, a place that is the romantic center of our nostalgic grip on fantasy. It is a powerful image of a prelapsarian past, one that became salient again in the 1980s in Reagan's representation of it. Reagan's biographers, including Gary Wills and Lou Cannon, have all noted in detail the contradiction between Reagan's "official" and public memories of his past and the actual fact of that past. It is easily provable that Reagan's representation of his own past is fictional, but that does not make it a deliberate and cynical lie; rather it makes his past a *popular past*, one that is enhanced and shared in the popular mind. He offered us an "improved" past that originated in popular culture as an idealization of what the country was supposed to remain to be forever. Reagan was not only an oracle, he was also a bard, a popular bard who was able to evoke, and even to embody, the nostalgic impulse and mood that makes us eschew history in exchange for myth. Reagan told us that we can go home again, and that there is a home to go to.

The history of North America is a restless one, with recurrent waves of immigration from abroad or migration within and the discovery of new frontiers at every turn. The myth of the immigrant who becomes an American is satisfying but still incomplete, since it involves foreign ties (as Michael Dukakis discovered) and urban settings that may be fearsome (as in contemporary "underclass" ghettoes). The myth of the frontier appeals to the pioneer spirit of adventure into the unknown but also has the dark underside of violent conquest and constant danger in an "unsettled" land. Reagan's mythic power stems from his identification with the Country, the settled land of the interior exemplified by the Town.

133

This is a more general myth that can encompass the other mythic strains in American life: in urban culture, the neighborhood becomes the model of the town, and on the frontier, the settlement is supposed to evolve from the wilderness into the model of civilization. The Town is forged out of the American genius for legitimate and "private" voluntary activities—family, church and business. The Town exists in the natural order of the Country, rooted in the eternal verities of familial devotion, religious harmony and business prosperity. It is a place in which it is always "morning in America," and the evils that had before beset humankind now were banished by the exceptional and distinctive American solution to the problem of civilization. The Town has the quality of Home, as a locale without the urbane attributes of cosmopolitanism and sophistication nor the savagery of the mean streets, and also devoid of the unsettled quality of the frontier. The Town is our mythic compromise, conserving the quality of American life on a human scale. If Reagan was a "conservative," it was at root in this sense: the conservation of a saving myth.

The politics of nostalgia has been attributed to many causes. There is no doubt that American life in the twentieth century has been fundamentally transformed by urbanization and the attendant shift not only of population but also of power to large cities and organizations. Reagan drew attention as a popular politician at precisely the time doubts about American mission and the inevitability of progress had become widespread. The American universe now seemed discontinuous, and traditional values and habits seemed more and more a thing of the past.

If our sense of an ordered world is indeed threatened, then the evocation of a saving myth by the right figure has an obvious appeal. It does not even matter much if the claims are phony or the appeal almost entirely symbolic: the nostalgic myth becomes a bulwark that cannot be recaptured, but it can be celebrated. "Reaganism" becomes not so much an ideology as a perspective, one that finds the image of the past as something that is at once a source of mythic strength but ironically also something that allows us contempt for the present and blind confidence in the future. The nostalgic perspective casts American life in the romantic mode of the personal, a locale with all the communal joys of a classless and conflict-free village, devoid of the relentless growth of the impersonal, in the late twentieth-century form of large organizational power that destroys through rational decision individual and community lives and indeed other nations and ultimately the Earth itself. Reagan in power was a willing part of that power structure, but he ruled, and we let him rule, through the mythic office of "returning the country around" toward those humane if archaic roots that somehow will result through the deconstruction of the welfare state and the flourishing of the warfare state. In the former domestic case, the nostalgic model had to be defended against the encroachments of organizational rationality that constitutes state intervention in the province of the personal, and in the latter foreign policy case, the portals of the Town had to be defended against these foreign forces, real or imagined, who would undermine its Edenic grace.

Political nostalgia, then, serves as a statement of faith in a changing world in which all faiths are challenged. A mythohistorical image gives us a temporal image to which the present may be unfavorably compared and to which we may even sporadically aspire. The various "back to nature," "back to basics" and "back to simplicity" movements which occurred in the wake of the upheavals of the 1960s were all rooted in this image, to which the American self, fearing the protean and antinomian strains on national identity, recurrently aspires. Such a widespread fear could only be partially allayed through consumption of nostalgic popular fare, or through the return to the country or small town and old houses; it also invited nostalgic politics that involved rhetorical invocation of those habits at the heart of the Country and somewhat more half-hearted attempts to reinvigorate, if not enforce, those habits thought to be the ethical base of the imaginary land. Against what Czech writer and politician Vaclav Havel has called the "eschatology of the impersonal," Reagan asserted against the Canutean tides of history and eschatology of the personal, a yearning for the tide to turn back to the future, or towards some future past that escapes the paradox of "prospective atavism" (Havel 27).

The Garden in the Machine

In the nineteenth- and early twentieth-century American past, the nostalgic myth helped people mediate the introduction of the machine in the garden. By the time of Reagan, as we entered the "post-industrial" world, the problem was one of saving the garden from the machine (Marx). On the one hand, this gave impetus to environmentalism, a movement that held on to a renewed version of the pastoral myth, one that was however futuristic, hoping to reform society by the restoration of nature and the ecotopian natural philosophy that should flow from it. But the Reaganesque ideal was contemptuous of environmentalism, since the image here was of a "natural society" in which the exploitation of nature never results in its depletion or exhaustion.

The economic machine both masters and is compatible with nature: "development" disturbs neither the social nor natural order. Indeed, it is here that the myth of progress emerges as a residue. Even though we may have grave doubts about progress, we still wish to believe that prospective atavism can somehow meld or control organizational power to the extent that the values and practices of the Town are restored or preserved. Progress may not seem as progressive as it once did, but if it is somehow incorporated into the nostalgic model, then the destructive bent that it has recently seemed to take is timed by the renewal of natural order.

For Reagan and his followers, the last prelapsarian period that offered hope of such a synthesis was the 1950s. (The second Reagan family actually lived in a General Electric model home in the 1950s.) The suburban movement seemed to offer hope that the Town could be transplanted in new communities in the Country surrounding the city with its attendant industrial and organizational plant. Bigness and anonymity could be defeated by location into a suburban complex, a small town in a green belt around big cities that were more and more industrial and immense. The impersonal could finally be defeated by the compromise of suburban life, a locale that offered the comforts of the village without the isolation of the "island community." The social and organizational machine could be held at bay in this respite from the complications of modernity. The pastoral garden had achieved in idyllic suburbia its American apotheosis, after which bourgeois aspiration should seek no more. There would be subsequent searches for a pastoral ideal (the hippie commune, the yuppie exurban) but in Reagan country the suburban way of life seemed the right fulfillment of the mythic heritage of the village. From it were banished all the ills that hitherto beset humankind, and in it were the latter-day versions of that institutional mix—family, church, business a short commute away—that deserved cultivation. The development of suburbia conquered both nature and the city, freeing the new

American from the labors of the farm and the boredom of the island community while also protecting him and her from the dangers and crowding of the city. It satisfied individual prospects while letting us retain our faith in an atavistic future.

By the late 1970s, however, the Reagan country of suburbia had suffered much criticism, and some of those who had aspired to the suburban ideal began to display doubts. The sense of entrapment, conformity and boredom and even hopelessness threatened the new pastoral ideal. Reagan reassured suburban dwellers and those who aspired to it that the critics were wrong and that where and how they lived was truly home in the traditions of Reagan country. Reagan had lived in both Town ideals, the Dixon of mythic memory and the General Electric home of the California days. In the former case, he was of the Midwest, the heartland of value and stability; in the latter case, he was of California, the quintessential land of opportunity, prosperity and sun-drenched leisure. He told those desperate to believe in the sanctity of their own quest and the quality of their own life that they were right and they were home. Their pursuit of happiness had ended, for they were in the American Dreamland safe and secure from all alarm. Do not despair, for you are in paradise.

The will to believe in the dreamscape of the American Garden was given political salience through Reagan's championship. For the constituents of the Town, it was useless, as always, to point to factualities such as statistics detailing the exclusivity of housing, since Reagan's appeal was mythic politics: what we, in our social ideal, wish ourselves as people to be. (The homeless, by contrast, served a useful mythic function: this is what happens to those who are not part of the Town nor have a Home.)

It was often said that Reagan presided over an imaginary state, a romantic land of shared make-believe. If the world that Reagan conjured was fictive in quotidian reality, it was quite salient in mythic reality, the higher truth to which he always appealed. His political epistemology dealt in the largest representational symbols, the warp and woof of popular knowledge. In that sense, he was not merely the head of state nor the head of government, he was more importantly the *head of populace*, presiding not only over ceremony and policy but also mythology. It is true that he was not universally popular, but for his constituency—those who saw themselves as denizens of Reagan country—he was the head of the "true" populace, those who saw themselves as the inhabitants of the Garden of the World. For them, the Garden could not, must not, turn into a nightmare.

The Fear of Learning

But the "terror of history" impinged on Reagan's time. The fear persisted that we were now in a postlapsarian world beyond recovery and redemption. The family, suburban and otherwise, continued to transform and often disintegrate; the business became an international rather than local enterprise; churches were beset by scandal and conflict over values. The unrelenting changes in American economic and political fortunes continued unabated. Reagan's considerable symbolic power could not alter the factualities of material power, as manifest in Japanese or European economic ascendancy. Reagan country could feel smug, but it also could feel scared. Our sense of mythic power could not renew dead factories, dying towns and auctioned farms. It is even argued that Reagan's mythic politics was a strategy of successfully managing domestic decline for internationally-minded economic elites.

In any case, Reagan pointed us once again toward the recertification of old forms and mythic aspirations. Such an orientation required that we not know certain kinds of political knowledge that might dispel the rediscovery of the Country. In Reagan country, popular knowledge consisted of settled truths of which Reagan the sage and oracle was the chief repository. The story of America had come to reside in the settlement of the Town and in the hearts of true Americans. It was a romance now consummated in a settled marriage, a place in which true knowledge is not in dispute. In that case, the American village calls not for disputation but certification, not doubt but faith, not individual thought but collective ritual. Reagan became for us the *popular hero as ritualist,* he who presided over the celebration of those things we know to be so and to be so forever. Reagan's celebrations of the eternal normalcy of true American life were ceremonies of innocence that offered hopeful sympathetic magic assuring us of the eternity of that life. He reminded us that myth is not false belief, but true belief, belief that required public resacralization.

This attitude toward knowledge helped define the curious ambivalence of Reagan's countrymen toward School. One might think that School would be a co-equal institution deserving the same ritual celebration accorded the Family, the Church and Business. Yet Reagan's rhetorical emphases—not to mention his budgets—gave only marginal attention to School. School was, to be sure, a part of the romantic mix of the nostalgic model, but as an instrument of knowledge it had become suspect.

In the Town, the School is supposed to be an extension of, and supporter of, Family, Church and Business. It is therefore a derivative institution, one that simply ratifies the settled truths of the Country. This includes patriotism, proper sex roles, private solutions and the mythic authority of benevolent local institutions. As part of a natural society, School is supposed to teach "natural education" that conforms with the settled principles of American localism. The skills and relationships learned there befit one for life in the Town, to teach critical thinking, objective history and universal or cosmopolitan values. (Reagan shared the popular notion that this educational innovation constituted teaching children "what to think," as if conservative drill did not.) The insistence by Reagan country to keep control of schools "local" implied a fear of learning, learning about things that undermined both the principle of localism and the primary knowledge that unquestioningly supported the locale of the Town. (Reagan as governor of California once insisted that his education at obscure Eureka College was much better than that received by those students at prestigious University of California-Berkeley, where, he darkly warned, the institution was engaged in "subsidizing intellectual curiosity.") By contrast, the School of Reagan country teaches a kind of unreflective athleticism (celebrated in the ritual of the sports banquet) and confident anti-intellectualism: "My grade school didn't have any books," Reagan boasted, "and look how I turned out."

Even though the local School is accorded a legitimate community function in the Reagan *mythos*, it is hard to escape the conclusion that school is suspect and indeed marginal for the proper functioning of the Town. This is because School cannot avoid its role in the propagation of learning, and that learning that goes beyond the pieties and principles of the Town is inherently subversive. (It is easy to think of Reagan as "pro-family," "pro-church" and "pro-business" in rhetorical emphases, but not "pro-school.") School threatened to teach us things about the unfolding world which alerted us to the nature of the postlapsarian world that was the terror of Reagan's history. Natural education at the local level could withstand a modicum of technological innovation, such as the computer, although even that was discomfiting enough, since technology separated children and then adults from their community; but it could not withstand educational innovation (with the rhetorical peroration of "social engineering") that was deemed an alienating force, separating school children from their natural condition, the wiser innocence of the Town. With the Reagan movement, School was something that had to be put in its proper place again, restored to basics that limited alternatives and horizons and reduced to its limited function in the harmony of the Town. As long as the School insisted that it was a repository of learning of no mythic or practical use to the Town, it remained an institution in a state of tension with Township normalcy. The fear of learning made the School something to be reckoned with, if local government in all its insularity and ignorance was to triumph.

The Decline of Authority

It was often said that Reagan ruled an imaginary state by practicing the magical art of seeming to make old dreams come true once again. In a sense, Reagan country did and did not exist. It existed as something nostalgic, but through prospective atavism could at least be recaptured momentarily in our dreams. It was as if Reagan was a political replay, satisfying our desire for "cultural repetition," as if the "limits of our popular experience have definitely been drawn, for we now look only for a verification of those limits—a recertification of old forms—rather than for a challenging of them, almost as if we have no more stories to tell, no new experiences to share." We are trying to "harden (our) myths" as a "static compendium of past motifs" (Graham 350). Reagan country is that compendium of past motifs hardened into a nostalgic myth for which we are wistful but also from which we draw political sustenance and even policy.

The reassertion of Reagan country, then, may well have been an historical defense, a social veneer of mythic protection from the relentlessness of change. Reagan did not ride an historical current; rather he found support in historical backwaters where change is puzzling and even terrifying. If symbolic politics is appropriate to periods of material and political decline of an aging empire, then he found it in the governing symbol of Reagan country. More subtly, he came to power in a century, and a country, suffering from the ongoing decline of authority. With traditional, legal-rational and charismatic authority all suspect, Reagan attempted to rule through another form: "mythic authority," rooted in the nostalgic image of the Country from which the present had fallen.

If historical meaning and continuity has been disturbed or ignored, then mythic meaning, both more consistent and reassuring, takes its place. Mythic learning means that one can proceed with the confidence of the sleepwalker, since historical learning has been relegated to the realm of unknowing, with its attendant lessons of failure, hardship, suffering and other harsh precedents. Mythic authority appeals not to tradition but rather folklore, displays contempt for the burgeoning and rule-governed bureaucracy of the legal-rational order and even eschews the transforming force of the charismatic leader. Reagan was not charismatic; rather we was a charmer, whose charm drew for us a magic circle of the atavistic past into which we could be drawn, making our world once again new and unspoiled. Such authority brings with it a sense of renewal from archaic and even primitive sources beyond historical experience, legalism and individual gift of grace. The "carrier" of myth is like the *hungan* who returns from an encounter with the gods to bring us their truth; it is, if believed, beyond dispute. For those imbued with the vision of Reagan country, he was a mythic authority whose artful representation of our mythic past was also beyond history, and in a sense, beyond politics. When the mythic authority announces the mystic knowledge that "America is back"— the past somehow mysteriously reclaimed by the gods for the present—then we are in the realm of an authoritative voice which bespeaks that knowledge that is at once the voice of god and of the people.

Those critics and satirists who thought Reagan's perspective was past-oriented and hopelessly roseate understood it as a form of naivete, a puerile stance that made it a form of infantile politics inadequate for the Machiavellian world. In its pragmatic applications, the nostalgic model is indeed so inadequate. But that was not its political function, even though Reagan himself, to the chagrin of his "pragmatic" advisors, often confused it. Reagan country is a mythic product not so much of political naivete as political sentimentalism, a popularly shared image of an elegiac world to be affirmed if not restored. Following Schiller, Isaiah Berlin has noted the distinction:

The unity [of the world] has been broken. The poet seeks to restore it. He looks for the vanished, harmonious world which some call nature, and builds it from his imagination, and his poetry is an attempt to return to it, to an imagined childhood, and he conveys his sense of the chasm which divides the day-to-day world which is no longer his home from the lost paradise which is conceived only ideally, only in reflection.

The elegiac "affirmation of the lost world, the unrealisable ideal" is "bounded by nothing; it is in its very essence indefinable, unattainable, incapable of being embraced by means of any finite medium, no matter how great the poet's capacity for finding, molding, transforming his material" (288-89). In "high culture," the art of sentiment finds many forms of expression, not all of them romantic or archaic; but in popular culture, the art of sentimentality often does combine nostalgic and romantic yearnings expressed in response to a disunified world that calls for restoration, or at least representation. Political elegiacs calls forth that world and declares its timelessness and timeliness. It may be an inaccessible "Elsewhere," but access to it calls us from after the Fall to which we are bound, but from which we wish to escape. If the future offers no exit, then all that is left is the past. But the only exit to the past is to build it from our present imagination, and that requires representation by a great popular artist who is able to communicate, and even embody, the certitude of the lost world.

Yet it appears that mythic authority, at least as exercised by Reagan, is ephemeral. Reagan was able to translate American "habits of the heart" into a vaguely familiar imaginative structure of nostalgic memory. Yet the major repositories of that memnotic experience in popular culture—prints and books, movies and television—are themselves subject to the force of time. When the nostalgic world of Reagan country no longer means anything to most people, they will abandon it for other models of the past— nostalgic for the rebellious 1960s, for instance, that gave so much impetus to Reagan and those who would recapture and even reimpose the past. The past, like the future, is always changing, always undergoing "revision" and acquiring new uses for the present. As Reagan country recedes as a viable memory, then other nostalgic images—such as the revolt of the 1960s—might well emerge as historical metaphor and exemplar. The populist and progressive strains would again require nostalgic basing in a mythic experience that gives it viability in a future present. The 1960s as nostalgic precedent could provide political action in that present with mythic authority, embodied by some political figure who is deemed the political representation of what that era meant and what it means for the present.

But if mythic authority is ephemeral, ultimately it is unstable. A future Reagan would experience quick passage in much the same way Reagan did after the Iran-contra affair and as his presidency wound down. Authority based on nostalgic yearnings and desires for restorative symbolism in a sense produce nothing substantial after the good feelings have passed. One has difficulty associating Reagan with anything lasting, such as a legislative program or structure of peace. Mythic authority seems to become politically viable in periods of great confusion and doubt following upheaval and failure. After the exercise in symbolic reassurance and assertion has spent itself, then it passes, as does the political figure who came to represent the impulse. There is no tradition to pass on, no legislative or executive agenda to implement, no charisma to routinize into a church or state, only the passing memory of someone who reminded us of popular myth dimly remembered and too often forgotten that can sustain us momentarily in a changing and uncertain present. In this sense, we may wonder whether Ronald Reagan was in fact truly a "conservative," since his political enactment seemed to conserve so little.

The Experience of Political Art

We may not wonder that Ronald Reagan was truly a great political artist. Mythic authority is an experience of art, the kind of art that gives imaginative life to those stories that give us roots which by extrapolation make sense of otherwise unintelligible things happening in our present lives. One of Reagan's greatest predecessors in Hollywood, the pioneering director D. W. Griffith, once predicted that whereas once we were as a people led by heroic warriors, and then led by the industrialist as hero, in the future we would replace the industrialist with the artist as popular hero. Indeed, he mused, "Perhaps motion pictures will do more to stimulate this interest than any other force" (Schickel, *D. W. Griffith* 467). Reagan learned how to be a popular hero as a movie artist who then expanded his career into political art. (It might also be argued that Reagan transformed the presidency into performance art.) The mythic quality in the movies, especially the nostalgic myth, translated well into political representation, so Reagan became the latter-day vessel of true popular belief.

The experience of political art is an aesthetic one, making Reagan first a student and then a master of political aesthetics. This is distinct from becoming a master of political power, which he exercised less skillfully and more reluctantly. At the end of our inquiry, we may also wonder if this is the wave of the political future, the substitution of aesthetic action for more familiar political action. Mythic politics requires aesthetic representation to succeed, but what the future of that kind of politics is remains to be seen. It may be that economic shocks will return us to a more substantial and less subtle period of material politics, based not in the poverty of symbolism but in the poverty of society. Mythic politics may be an amusing luxury of an affluent but morally ambivalent society not sure where it is going and wishing to know, or to return to, where it has been. Deep economic travail by contrast focuses the mind wonderfully.

Nevertheless, we may also end by speculating that Reagan's popular success indicates a malaise in the national spirit that he came to power to deny, but which persists in spite of (or because of) him. Mythic politics may then not solve anything in the long run, and after our spirits have been momentarily lifted, they then fall again in the wake of the disappearance of political ephemera, like ghosts at dawn. As the movies themselves have long portrayed, there has always been an America of darker and plainer myth than the nostalgic myth Reagan embraced as the singular message of the movies (Thomson). As we near the twenty-first century, the nostalgic myth we inherited from the nineteenth century may reach a point of mythic inadequacy. We may suspect that the future will look upon Reagan country, both in fact and fiction, as specific to a previous age, and that new myth will emerge from the political ashes of old, in the ongoing American search for popular meaning.

Ronald Reagan made nostalgia into a political art, an art that gave representative life to our fear that we have lost something important and that we cannot ever regain what we have lost. It is in this sense that an elaborate exercise in political nostalgics may in the last analysis be mythically inadequate. For nostalgia is a mythic referent that no longer exists (if it ever did), a time and place to which we cannot go home again. By exalting the model of the past, nostalgia makes it over into something that we may fear we have lost, but which is ultimately frustrating because we cannot ever regain it. Nostalgic politics is in that way a denial of history, and even more fundamentally, a denial of process, that times goes on and so do the processes of history. Nostalgia breeds self-satisfaction, as if the present and the future will take care of itself if only we celebrate, and mythologize, the past. As Lasch reminds us, "...a sense of continuity is exactly what nostalgia discourages" (69). With that orientation, it is no wonder that the American garden was untended during the Reagan years, threatening to turn the American future into a desert. Nostalgia doesn't require action, since it lets us believe that what we have to recapture is the past, not anticipate the future. It is not the future the nostalgic artist anticipates; rather it is the past. The triumph of political nostalgia then does rob us of any sense of historical continuity. Nostalgia allays our fears that we lost something important, but beyond that it does little more. Nostalgia speaks to fears, not hopes. Hope can only be raised through a vision of the future, and that requires a sense of historical continuity leading us to a brighter future. Following in the footsteps of Reagan, George Bush had great difficulty with "the vision thing," and no wonder: the ruling myth of the regime established by Reagan allowed no futuristic vision. Its political sentiments accorded glory and honor to past achievements and past precedents and steadfastly attempted to turn the clock back or deny the necessity for planning for the future. Meanwhile, the processes of history—the shift in global economics, the depletion of the environment, the atrophy of democracy and political participation at home—continued unabated since they were unrecognized.

Political nostalgia, then, augured a kind of political death, since it seemed to preclude foresight and vision and any kind of innovative political learning. An adequate new myth would have to come from somewhere outside established ruling circles, who seemed resolute in the maintenance of their political ignorance. Reagan Country would face the new century in the rusting armor of past glories and past certainties, blissfully unaware that in the long run, we and our myths are all dead. The success of political nostalgia means that we are afraid of the future and seek instead the comforts of a mythic past translated into political art. The twenty-first century, however, is likely not to be a future in which a mythic national past will be adequate for survival.

Notes

Introduction

[1]Alexis de Tocqueville, *Democracy in America* (many editions); recent use of Tocqueville includes Richard Reeves, *American Journey* (New York: Simon and Schuster, 1982); Robert N. Bellah and associates, *Habits of the Heart* (Berkeley: U of California P, 1985); Raymond Aron, *Main Currents in Sociological Thought, I* (Garden City, NY: Doubleday Anchor, 1968); Roger C. Boesche, "The Strange Liberalism of Alexis de Tocqueville," *History of Political Thought* 2 (Winter 1981): 495-524; Boesche, "Why Could Tocqueville Predict so Well?" *Policitical Theory* 11.1 (Feb. 1983): 79-103; Catherine H. Zuckert, "Reagan and That Unnamed Frenchman (de Tocqueville): On the Rationale for the New (Old) Federalism," *Review of Politics* 45 (July 1983): 421-42.

[2]See, for leading analyses, such works as R. W. B. Lewis, *The American Adam* (Chicago: U of Chicago P, 1955); Max Lerner, *America as a Civilization* (New York: Simon and Schuster, 1957); Robert Benne and Phillip Hefner, *Defining America* (Philadelphia: Fortress, 1974); Ernest Lee Tuveson, *Redeemer Nation* (Chicago: U of Chicago P, 1968); Wilfred L. Guerin, et al, "Myth Criticism and the American Dream," *A Hanedbook of Critical Approaches to Literature* (New York: Harper and Row, 1979) 185-191; Patrick Gerster and Nichols Cords, *Myth in American History* (Encino, CA: Glenco, 1977); H. Mark Roelofs, *Ideology and Myth in American Politics* (Boston: Little, Brown, 1976); Leo Marx, *The Machine in the Garden* (New York: Oxford UP, 1964); Seymour Martin Lipset, *The First New Nation* (New York: Norton, 1979); Henry Nash Smith, *The Virgin Land* (New York: Vintage, 1950); Robert Jewett, *The Captain America Complex* (Philadelphia: Westminster, 1973); Robert Jewett and John Shelton Lawrence, *The American Monomyth* (Garden City, NY: Doubleday Anchor, 1977); Dan Nimmo and James Combs, *Subliminal Politics* (Englewood Cliffs, NJ: Prentice-Hall, 1980).

[3]Cf. Richard Slotkin, *Regeneration through Violence* (Middletown: Wesleyan UP, 1973); D. H. Lawrence, *Studies in Classic American Literature* (New York: Viking, 1964); Frederic I. Carpenter, *America Literature and the Dream* (New York: Philosophical Library, 1955); Carpenter, " 'The American Myth': Paradise to be Regained," *PML.1* 74 (Dec. 1959): 559-606; John Adair, *Founding Fathers: The Puritans and America* (London: Dent, 1982).

Works Cited

Annenberg, Walter H. "The Case for President Reagan." *TV Guide* 6 Oct. 1984.

Baas, Larry. "Ronald Reagan and the Gender Gap." *The Cresset* 57.5 (March 1984): 10-13.

Barton, Bruce. *The Man Nobody Knows.* NY: Bobbs-Merrill, 1924.

Berger, Peter L. *The Sacred Canopy.* Garden City, NY: Doubleday Anchor, 1969.

Berlin, Isaiah. "The 'Naivete' of Verdi." *Against the Current.* New York: Penguin, 1982.

Brown, Norman O. *Love's Body.* New York: Vintage, 1966.

Cannon, Lou. *President Reagan: The Role of a Lifetime.* New York: Simon and Schuster, 1991.

Caughey, John L. "Artificial Social Relations in Modern America." *American Quarterly* 30 (1978): 70-89.

Cawelti, John. "Pornography, Catastrophe, and Vengeance: Shifting Narrative Structures in a Changing American Culture." *The American Self.* Ed. Sam B. Girgus. Albuquerque: U of New Mexico P, 1981. 181-92.

Chicago Tribune. 24 Oct. 1984.

Context. DuPont. 13.3 (1984).

Dallek, Robert. *Ronald Reagan: The Politics of Symbolism.* Cambridge: Harvard UP, 1984.

Dixon, Greg. Speech. Executive Secretary for the National Moral Majority. Open Door Baptist Church, Valparaiso, IN. 16 Jan. 1981.

Easterbrook, Gregg. "The Republican Soul." *The Washington Monthly* July/Aug. 1981.

Ewen, Stuart. *Captains of Consciousness.* New York: McGraw-Hill, 1976.

Fiedler, Leslie. *Love and Death in the American Novel.* Cleveland: Meridan, 1960.

Fisher, Walter R. "Romantic Democracy, Ronald Reagan, and Presidential Heroes." *Western Journal of Speech Communication.* 46 (Summer 1982).

Friedman, Robert. "Inspiration, Inc." *Esquire* Sept. 1979.

Furay, Conal. *The Grass-Roots Mind in America: The American Sense of Absolutes.* New York: Franklin Watts New Directions, 1977.

Galbraith, John Kenneth. *The Great Crash, 1929.* Boston: Houghton Mifflin, 1972.

Gitlin, Todd. *The Whole World is Watching.* Berkeley: U of California P, 1980.

Goldman, Eric F. *Rendezvous with Destiny.* New York: Vintage, 1956.

Gorer, Geoffrey. *The American People.* New York: Norton, 1964.

Graham, Allison. "History, Nostalgia, and the Criminality of Popular Culture." *Georgia Review* 38.2 (Summer 1984).

Griswold, J. "I'm a Sucker for Hero Worship." *New York Times Book Review* 86 (30 Aug. 1981).

Guerin, Wilfred L., et al. "Myth Criticism and the American Dream." *A Handbook of Critical Approaches to Literature*. New York: Harper and Row, 1979.

Gusfield, Joseph. *Symbolic Crusade*. Urbana: U of Illinois P, 1969.

Hart, Roderick P. *The Political Pulpit*. West Lafayette, IN: Purdue UP, 1977.

Havel, Vaclav. "The Regime Within." *Harper's* June 1986.

Hofstadter, Richard. *The Age of Reform*. New York: Vintage, 1955.

_____ *The American Political Tradition*. New York: Vintage, 1974.

Horsefield, Peter G. *Religious Television: The American Experience*. New York: Longman, 1984.

Jewett, Robert and John Lawrence. "American Civil Religion and Ritual Blindness." *The Christian Century* 23 Nov. 1983: 1075-78.

Kammen, Michael. *People of Paradox*. New York: Vintage, 1973.

Klapp, Orrin E. *Collective Search for Identity*. New York: Holt, Rinehart and Winston, 1969.

_____ *Symbolic Leaders*. n.p.: Minerva, 1968.

Kornhauser, William. *The Politics of Mass Society*. New York: Free, 1969.

Kretch, David, et al. *Individual in Society*. New York: McGraw-Hill, 1962.

Lasch, Christopher. "The Politics of Nostalgia." *Harper's* Nov. 1984.

Leamer, Laurence. *Make-Believe: The Story of Nancy and Ronald Reagan*. New York: Harper and Row, 1983.

Lewis, R. W. B. *The American Adam*. Chicago: U of Chicago P, 1955.

Lewis, Sinclair. *Babbitt*. New York: Harcourt, Brace and World, 1922.

Lowenthal, Leo. *Literature, Popular Culture, and Society*. Englewood Cliffs, NJ: Prentice-Hall, 1961.

Maines, David R., et al. "The Sociological Import of G. H. Mead's Theory of the Past." *American Sociological Review* 48 (April 1983): 161-173.

Marty, Martin E. "Religious Television: A Challenge Unmet." *Christian Century* 12-19 Sept. 1984.

Marx, Leo. *The Machine in the Garden*. New York: Oxford UP, 1964.

May, Henry F. *The End of American Innocence*. Chicago: Quadrange, 1964.

May, Lary. *Screening out the Past*. Chicago: U of Chicago P, 1983.

Mead, George Herbert. *The Philosophy of the Present*. Chicago: U of Chicago P, 1980.

Meyerowitz, Joshua. *No Sense of Place*. New York: Oxford UP, 1985.

Mondale, Walter. Campaign Mail-out Letter. Democratic Campaign Headquarters, 1984.

Neuhaus, Richard John. *The Naked Public Square*. Grand Rapids, MI: Eerdman's, 1984.

Nisbet, Robert. *The Sociological Tradition*. New York: Basic, 1966.

Pitkin, Hannah. *The Concept of Representation*. Berkeley: U of California P, 1967.

Pope, Carl. "Ronald Reagan and the Limits of Responsibility." *Sierra* May/June 1984: 51-54.

Ray, Robert B. *A Certain Tendency of the Hollywood Cinema, 1930-1980*. Princeton: Princeton UP, 1985.

Reagan, Ronald. Preface. *Norman Rockwell's Patriotic Times*. By George Mendoza. New York: Viking, 1985.

_____ Introduction. *Surrender in Panama*. By Phillip M. Crane. New York: Dale, 1978.

Rogin, Michael. "Ronald Reagan's American Gothic." *Democracy* 1 (Oct. 1981).

Rollins, Peter C. "Will Rogers and the Relevance of Nostalgia: Steamboat Round the Bend." *American History/American Film*. Eds. John E. O'Connor and Martin A. Jackson. New York: Frederick Ungar, 1980.

Schickel, Richard. *D. W. Griffith: An American Life*. New York: Simon and Schuster, 1984.

_____ "Fairbanks: His Picture in the Papers." *Celebrity*. Ed. James Monaco. New York: Dell, 1978. 121-127.

_____ *Intimate Strangers: The Culture of Celebrity*. Garden City, NY: Doubleday, 1985.

Schwartz, Barry. *George Washington*. New York: Free, 1987.

Sklar, Robert. "God and Man in Bedford Falls: Frank Capra's 'It's a Wonderful Life'." *The American Self*. Ed. Sam R. Girgus. Albuquerque: U of New Mexico P, 1981. 211-220.

_____ *Movie-Made America*. New York: Vintage, 1975.

Slosser, Bob. *Reagan Inside Out*. Waco, TX: Word Books, 1984.

Thomson, David. *Suspects*. New York: Knopf, 1985.

Timms, Ed. "Abbie Hoffman's Plaint: 'These kids today'..." *Chicago Tribune* (12 Oct. 1984) sec. 2:4.

Towner, Lawrence J. "The City on a Hill." *An American Primer*. Ed. Daniel J. Boorstin. New York: Mentor, 1968.

"University Students Support Reagan." *CSP* release, 28 Oct. 1984.

van Damm, Helen, ed. *Sincerely, Ronald Reagan*. New York: Berkeley, 1980.

Veblin, Thornstein. *The Theory of the Leisure Class*. New York: Funk and Wagnalls, n.d.

Vidich, Arthur J. and Joseph Bensman. *Small Town in Mass Society*. Garden City, NY: Doubleday Anchor, 1960.

Ward, John William. *Andrew Jackson: Symbol for an Age*. New York: Oxford UP, 1955.

_____ "The Meaning of Lindbergh's Flight." *American Quarterly* 10.1 (1958): 3-16.

Wecter, Dixon. *The Hero in America*. New York: Scribner, 1941.

Wertheim, Arthur Frank. "Relieving Social Tensions: Radio Comedy and the Great Depression." *Journal of Popular Culture* 10:3 (1976) 501-519.

Wills, Gary. *Cincinnatus: George Washington and the Enlightenment*. Garden City, NY: Doubleday, 1984.

_____ *Reagan's America: Innocents at Homes*. Garden City, NY: Doubleday, 1987.

Wolfe, Tom. "The 'Me Decade' and the Third Great Awakening." *New York* 23 Aug. 1976: 26-40.

Wolfenstein, Martha. "The Emergence of Fun Morality." *Journal of Social Issues* 7 (1951): 10-15.

Wolfenstein, Martha and Nathan Leites. *Movies: A Psychological Study*. Glencoe, IL: Free, 1950.

Woodward, Kenneth L. and Elizabeth Bailey. "Who's a 'Good Christian'?" *Newsweek* 6 Aug. 1984.

Worthington, Rogers. "Terrorism: Mindless Violence or New International Politics?" *Chicago Tribune* 29 Nov. 1979: Sec. 2: 1, 3.

Wyllie, Irving. *The Self-Made Man in America.* New Brunswick, NJ: Rutgers UP, 1954.

about the author

James Combs is a professor of political science at Valparaiso University in Indiana. He belongs to that exclusive field within that profession and discipline who specialize in the study of the relationship between popular culture and politics.